Beginning Our Day

Volume Two

Dhamma Reflections from Abhayagiri Monastery

Abhayagiri Buddhist Monastery
16201 Tomki Road
Redwood Valley, California 95470
www.abhayagiri.org
707-485-1630

Interior design by Suhajjo Bhikkhu. Cover design by Sumi Shin.
Cover photos by Jonathan Payne.

We would like to acknowledge the support of the Kataññutā group of
Malaysia, Singapore, and Australia for bringing this book into full
production.

Printed using paper from a sustainable source.

sabbadānaṃ dhammadānaṃ jināti.
The gift of Dhamma excels all gifts.

This book is dedicated to our teachers and parents.

Contents

Preface

"Beginning our day ..."

These quintessential words are spoken by Luang Por
Pasanno before he begins each of his morning reflections.

Five days a week, at Abhayagiri's morning meeting, work
tasks are assigned to the residents and guests living in the
monastery. Shortly thereafter, one of the senior monks offers a
brief Dhamma reflection so that the residents and guests have
something meaningful to recollect throughout their day.

These talks are given spontaneously and often address an
event that is about to occur, a condition that is already present
in the monastery, or a general teaching on Dhamma. The most
common thread through all the reflections is that of practi-
cality: distilling the most important teachings of the Buddha
into pertinent and applicable practices. Though many different
teachings are touched upon, the fundamental aim is to encourage the abandonment of the unwholesome, the cultivation of
the wholesome, and the purification of the mind.

While several of these teachings may be read together at
one time, readers might find it more useful to focus on a single
reflection so they can easily recollect, contemplate, and make
use of it throughout their day.

This book was made possible through the contributions
of many people. More than ten years ago, Pamela Kirby ini-
tiated the project when she placed a recorder in front of one
of the senior monks during a morning reflection and pro-
posed that a book be written. Matthew Grad, Jeff Miller, Ila

Lewis, Ray Peterson, and Laurent Palmatier were the main substantive editors of the material, enduring the long and difficult process of editing the transcripts into compact and well-written teachings. Pamela Kirby generously offered assistance at various stages of the editing process. Ruby Grad helped with the copy editing. Shirley Johannesen helped with the glossary. David Burrowes, Dee Cope, Josh Himmelfarb, Evan Hirsch, Jeanie Daskais, Anagārika John Nishinaga, and members of the Lotus Volunteer Group: Wendy Parker and Viveka all helped with further refining of the text. Sumi Shin designed the cover. Jonathan Payne took the cover photos. Michael Smith tumbled the stones for the back cover.

For several years, Khemako Bhikkhu recorded the senior monks' reflections. Kovilo Bhikkhu and Pesalo Bhikkhu provided corrections on an early draft of the book. Suhajjo Bhikkhu generously dedicated a significant amount of time on the overall book design and typesetting of the text.

The Collected Teachings of Ajahn Chah published by Aruna Publications in 2011 provided many of the terms in the glossary.

The Kataññutā group of Malaysia, Singapore, and Australia generously brought this book into full production.

Any errors that remain in these reflections are my own responsibility.

May these teachings bring insight into the nature of Dhamma and provide a pathway toward the development of true peace and contentment.

Cunda Bhikkhu
Abhayagiri Monastery
May 2014

Abbreviations

DN   Dīgha Nikāya
MN   Majjhima Nikāya
SN   Saṃyutta Nikāya
AN   Aṅguttara Nikāya
Sn   Sutta Nipāta
Cp   Cariyāpiṭaka
Jā   Jātaka

Avoiding the Second Arrow

Luang Por Pasanno • November 2013

The obvious thing for me right now is carrying this cold around: a thick head and not much energy. It's helpful to reflect on the reality of illness or discomfort that is natural and happens all the time. What comes to mind is the Buddha's discourse on the two arrows. Being struck by one arrow is painful, and being struck by a second one is painful as well. In terms of feeling, because each of us has a body, it is quite natural that we experience unpleasant sensations. And due to having a mind, it is also natural that we are sensitive to the sense contacts we experience. These are qualities of the first arrow. Becoming averse, worried, or anxious about unpleasant feeling or planning and proliferating about how to escape from sense contact, is the second arrow.

We can't avoid the first arrow, but we can avoid the second arrow. Because we have physical bodies, because we exist, our bodies naturally get ill and our minds change. There are always going to be certain elements of unpleasant feelings. Even the Buddha himself experienced unpleasant feelings and had physical ailments, like a bad back. There are places in the suttas where the Buddha turns over his teaching role to either Ānanda or Sāriputta because his back is too sore to continue sitting and teaching.

We can recognize and be attentive to the first arrow and not turn that arrow into something that then creates more complication, difficulty, and pain. We can reflect on that as we go about the day, asking ourselves, *What are my reactions to unpleasant feelings? What are my habits and tendencies?* We can develop mindfulness and discernment to receive the first arrow skillfully and not look for ways to be struck by the second, third, or fourth arrow.

The Importance of
Koṇḍañña's Insight

Ajahn Amaro • November 2008

In the Dhammacakkapavatana Sutta, the Discourse on the Turning of the Wheel of Dhamma, the Buddha addressed the five *samaṇas*, including one named Koṇḍañña, who were his practice companions before he became a Buddha. At the end of this talk, the Buddha recognized that Koṇḍañña had, with deep insight, understood the Dhamma. He said, *"Aññāsi vata bho Koṇḍañño, aññāsi vata bho Koṇḍañño ti*—Koṇḍañña understands, Koṇḍañña understands." Koṇḍañña had awakened to the nature of Dhamma: *"Dhammacakkhuṃ udapādi*—the eye of Dhamma arose." Then the sutta describes exactly what it was that Koṇḍañña saw. It wasn't a spectacular vision of the heavens opening up, a bewildering light display that he experienced, or streams of deities beaming down from the heavens. Rather, his vision of the Dhamma was stated simply in the phrase, *"Yaṅkiñci samudayadhammaṃ sabbantaṃ nirodhadhamman ti*—whatever is subject to arising is subject to ceasing."

On a worldly level this seems completely unremarkable: That which begins, ends. Whatever goes up, must come down. If it's born, it dies. *No big deal,* we might think. But it's worth our reflection: This seemingly simple insight, which makes all the difference in the life of Koṇḍañña, which enables him to awaken to the Dhamma, enter into the stream of Dhamma, and make full enlightenment absolutely certain from that point on—why should that be the most profound insight?

It's helpful to reflect on this and use it as a theme of meditation. *Why would it change my life to see that all that is subject to arising is subject to ceasing? If that's truly known and understood by me, why should that mean that full enlightenment is inevitable, that in a certain amount of time it will ripen in my complete and total liberation? How can that understanding be so important?* We can practice picking up that theme, applying it, and seeing it clearly for ourselves. It's not simply a collection of words that we hear, *Oh yeah, "All that's subject to arising is subject to ceasing." Yeah, I know all that.* We can practice exploring it and applying it, moment by moment, throughout the day. *Why should that be so liberating? Why should that be so significant? Why should that be the change of vision that alters my whole way of life, my whole way of seeing who and what I am?* This is for all of us to investigate.

When we apply this insight to everything—to what we think, to what we feel, to the pleasant experiences, the painful experiences, the beautiful, the ugly, the emotionally pleasing, the emotionally distressing—it awakens a sense of the nature of experience itself. We begin to see that when we aren't judging life in worldly terms—good, bad, right, wrong, me, you, beautiful, ugly, in here, out there—then we're seeing everything in terms of its nature, rather than its content or whether we like it or we don't like it, whether we call it in here or out there. We awaken to that intuition within us that everything internal and external, mental and physical, is part of a natural order. It's not self. It's not who or what we are. It's not personal. It's not alien. It's just Dhamma. It's nature itself. This understanding undercuts the way we see ourselves as, "Me in here, the world out there." We no longer believe that those perceptions reflect the way things truly are.

This insight seems like nothing, doesn't it? Our ego-centered thinking reacts like it's oxygen: *Big deal. There's a lot of oxygen about, so what?* But when we are denied oxygen, then it quickly becomes apparent how crucial it is. In a similar way, when we apply this insight to how we experience our thoughts, feelings, and perceptions, then it changes the whole way we hold things. We can notice that change within the heart. *Oh right, this is a changing thing. I can call it good or bad. I can call it success or failure. But its primary quality is that it's changing. It came into being and now it's ending. That's the most important thing about it.* We notice that shift in the heart, that shift that happens within us when we apply Koṇḍañña's insight. It changes everything because we're no longer obsessing—fixating on the content of experience. We're becoming aware of the process of experience itself.

That's fundamentally what insight, *vipassanā*, is about. Vipassanā is insight into the nature of experience itself—that moment of clear seeing when there's a direct awareness of how experience works, what experience is. And the result of that is liberation. At that moment the heart knows, *This is merely a pattern of nature, a coming, a going—changing. That's all it is. That's all it can be. Nothing to get excited about. Nothing to get alarmed about.* Right there is the moment of freedom in seeing clearly that the heart is unburdened. There is an unentangled knowing, at least to some small degree. That liberating quality is right here, in the midst of everyday activity, mundane thoughts, and feelings. Just like Koṇḍañña, it is possible for us to access this liberating insight right here and right now.

Refocusing on the Defilements

Ajahn Yatiko • May 2012

One of the problems we come across is the tendency to forget the goal of our practice and life—in other words, the direction where we should be aiming. We need to frequently return to the basic intention to be free from the defilements of greed, hatred, and delusion, because it's so easy to get caught up in the conditions of daily life, wanting the conditions to be a certain way, either liking our present conditions or disliking them. People who are active, work a lot, coordinate a lot, or do a lot of planning can easily spend the whole day manipulating conditions, especially if they are skilled at this.

I once knew a German monk in Thailand who candidly said to me that he could look at anything, for instance a water fountain, and tell me five things that were wrong with it. He said he could look at anything and tell me how to improve it, whether it's in the wrong place, designed poorly, or not properly cared for. He said this in a sweet, non-boasting way. It's easy for people with that ability to believe that they can sort out all the conditions. Sometimes things truly aren't working well or people aren't behaving the way they should, and in our minds we think we can get it all sorted out. But when we try, it doesn't usually work out the way we want. Or if it does, that can be even worse, because then we're not likely to have been aware of the defilements that came up when we attached to our view about the right way of doing things.

It's as if we have a spotlight of awareness focused on external conditions, applying strong views and judgments about the way things are or should be. This can create a great amount of suffering in some cases. Basically, we're looking in the wrong place. We can spend our whole lives focusing outward, trying to get things, situations, or people to do what we want, forgetting that our awareness and perception should be focused inwardly, on ourselves. In our tradition it's been said that as monastics 95 percent of our focus should be on our own state of mind, our own movements of mind. We focus internally because we want to be free from suffering and this is how we accomplish this task.

Not long ago we drove up to the Old Gold Mine Hermitage and in the van I listened to a classic talk from Ajahn Jayasāro. It's called "Recognizing the Upakkilesas." In this talk, he analyzes various defilements of the mind such as anger, ill will, cruelty, envy, belittling, and self-righteousness. As I listened, a mood of irritation came up, and I started investigating what this irritation could be and how I could describe its nature. To really describe a defilement we need to study it. For me, it's not so helpful to study defilements intellectually, as in the Visuddhimagga, where each defilement is defined as having specific attributes and proximate causes. Instead, the way of study I find most helpful in practice is through direct experience. So with irritation, for example, we study what's going on right now, once irritation has arisen. We investigate what it's all about, what it feels like, and what conditions gave rise to it in this specific case. Doing this, we can clearly see that the conditions which gave rise to irritation will change, and that irritation will arise again in another situation if those same conditions are present.

We can use whatever arises as an object of study. Taking an extreme hypothetical situation, let's say an anagārika calls me "Ajahn Fatico," and I get upset about this, thinking what he said was inappropriate and insulting. Let's say this gives rise to anger, and I really want to set him straight. However, in terms of my own practice, the fact that he insulted me is not the point at all because even if I do set him straight and he apologizes, in the future I may feel hurt or angered by a comment somebody else makes—I've done nothing to prevent that hurt and anger from arising when the same conditions recur. It's an endless cycle for us if we go about things in this way. So we need to change our focus from being set on external conditions, such as what other people say and do, and instead focus on the way our attachments, cravings, and defilements move through experience. We can see that they aren't ours—they don't belong to us. We need to recognize and appreciate that.

The Pāli word *āgantuka* means newcomer or guest. An āgantuka monk is a visiting monk who comes from a different tradition, who may have different standards of Vinaya, or who does not know the way we do things here. In one sutta passage, the Buddha says that the defilements are visitors—that the mind is intrinsically pure, and the defilements come into the mind as āgantuka (AN 1.49). So the defilements are merely visitors, they don't really belong in the mind. We have to see how these defilements arise and pass away, how they're not part of us and don't define who we are. To see that takes attention, focus, and a clear sense of what our priorities are in the practice.

One Breath at a Time

Luang Por Pasanno • June 2012

Distributing the daily work assignments seemed a bit complicated today. That's the nature of organizing many people living together. When there is one person living in one place, it's fairly simple. With two people it's a little harder, and it gets exponentially more complicated as the number of people increases.

For this reason, we need to learn the skills of living together, so that our own interactions and how we relate to each other don't get overly complicated. In general terms, as practitioners, it is essential that we cultivate the quality of simplicity in the ways we relate to things. In reality, there is one moment at a time, and we take one step at a time when we do things. It's not all that complicated.

But the mind tends to leap forward toward proliferation, so we need the patience to step back and ask ourselves, *What do I have to deal with right now?* Mostly all we have to deal with right now is breathing in and breathing out. There's not much to do. If there is a task to be done, then we can learn how to apply patience and attention to it. We put attention on what we are doing, the way it impacts the people around us, and the circumstances we are in.

As we do this, we realize that the morning has passed, another day has moved on. Very simple. We can recall this quality of simplicity as we pay attention to the reactions in the mind, the moods that keep popping up, and the proliferations that keep hounding us. We can remember: *One breath at a time, one step at a time.* It's all very uncomplicated and there's not much to be done.

Brightening the Mind

Ajahn Karuṇadhammo • August 2012

Recent discussions and Dhamma talk reflections have focused on the theme of right effort. Many of us can be so caught up in what we think of as Dhamma practice or meditation practice that we create a narrow focus for ourselves. Several of us here came to Buddhism with a focus on the practice of meditation in the context of silent retreat, oftentimes with a very specific technique related to quieting the mind. Sometimes it's easy to get the idea that Buddhist practice boils down to right concentration or a specific meditation method. But the Buddha's Eightfold Path is much broader than that. Right effort, one of these path factors, is a significant skill to be developed. With right effort, we are learning to be sensitive to the effect our minds have on what it is we're doing. We are examining and asking ourselves, *Are wholesome states increasing or unwholesome states decreasing?* That's our benchmark. That's our measure of whatever it is we're doing in what we call our Buddhist practice.

For instance, the theme today for Upāsikā Day, "Brightening the Mind," focuses on the formal side of meditation, which is often—but not explicitly—talked about in terms of contemplation. There are many kinds of active reflections the Buddha gave to help prepare, brighten, and soften the mind. By building on those qualities we can develop more refined states of concentration. So that is our orientation—to learn how to develop and prepare the mind, not only with formal meditation practice, but also in our daily activities.

The rest of the path is oriented toward the other supports and developments of right view and the attitudes and actions that are part and parcel of our practice to liberate the mind. We follow this path by paying attention to whatever it is we are doing, in the livelihood we've chosen and in the activities and various ways we express ourselves in body, speech, and mind. We can ask ourselves if what we are doing or thinking is leading toward wholesome states of mind—toward more peace, contentment, and satisfaction, or toward less stress, suffering, clinging, and holding on to unskillful habits of responding in the world. We can use that as the benchmark around all of our activities, everything we do. This in turn allows us to let go of the belief that meditation or practice is something we do only after our activities are done, when we get up to our *kuṭis* or find a place to sit quietly. We are gaining insight into the perspective that it's all practice right here and right now, toward the increasing of wholesome mind states and the decreasing of unwholesome ones.

The Benefits and Drawbacks of Change

Luang Por Pasanno • October 2012

There is a feeling of change today since the rain has come. The rain on the roof is an unfamiliar sound after months and months of dry summer. As I came down this morning for *pūjā*, there was the smell of moisture in the air. We can pay attention to that feeling of change.

The mind tends to look at things from a one-sided perspective. We might be people who love the warm summer and hate the cold rainy time, or we might like the colder wet weather and hate the heat. But nothing is ever one-sided like that. Everything has its benefits and drawbacks, and the Buddha instructs us to investigate that.

This includes investigating the drawbacks of things we like and are excited about. It's starting to get cool, the dust has settled, the plants are coming out, and the forest is regenerating—these are the benefits of this lovely weather. At the same time, a gutter is leaking, and water is dripping down the side of a wall onto a deck and needs to be repaired.

There was a group of Pa-Auk Sayadaw's lay disciples who were planning on coming up today to have a look at Abhayagiri. They were thinking about how to develop their new property for Pa-Auk and were excited to see what we've done here. However, we received an email from them this morning saying that with the new rain they found leaks in several of their buildings and need to fix them right away. So they have to postpone their trip for some time.

There are benefits and drawbacks to everything. If we think in terms of, *I like this* or *I don't like that,* we end up trapping ourselves. By looking at experience from a broader perspective and applying Dhamma to it, we can more easily recognize that everything has two or more sides and see more clearly how problematic it is to take a personal position on what we are experiencing. That way we're not investing in the "I, me, and mine" sense of how we think things should be. Rather, we're examining the way things are, reflecting on both the benefits and drawbacks of the situation.

Snow on a Forest Trail

Ajahn Jotipālo • December 2013

This morning I was walking through the forest on a path that I've walked thousands of times before, and everything looked completely different. Two conditions had changed: there was moisture in the air and the temperature had dropped below freezing. This completely transformed the path. Most of the trees were covered with heavy snow and ice. It was quite beautiful.

I was contemplating this in terms of the characteristic of not-self, as a reminder of how we can take our thoughts, moods, and opinions and believe them to be who and what we are. We may have a thought and then some reaction, like anger, but that anger is not who we are—it's merely a transient phenomenon, like the snow on the trail. It's merely the result of some condition that came into being. Whatever habitual reactions we may have, they have been conditioned into us. They're all due to past causes. And just like snow will melt given a certain temperature, when the conditions change for us, our reactions may change as well.

I used to be bothered by a couple of people in the community, the way they habitually reacted in certain situations. Then one day it hit me that those people were merely reacting exactly as they'd been conditioned to react in that particular situation. This has given me a lot of space around difficult interactions that occur with other people, and I've been able to recondition my own habitual reactions. When I experience aversion to somebody, I can think to myself, *If they could act differently they would act differently.* Or I might also think, *When the conditions change, this may no longer be their habitual reaction.* It can be that impersonal.

This is something we all can do. When we encounter a situation with that sort of wisdom, we can respond with compassion, equanimity, and understanding, and not experience the *dukkha* of aversion. We can transform our inner landscape, as with the snow fallen on a forest trail.

The Dhamma of the Buddha Is Everywhere

Luang Por Pasanno • May 2012

As we engage in activity, we can ground our awareness in the body and use it as a helpful anchor for our practice. We do this by having a tactile sense of contact with the ground, contact with physical movement, and contact with the material world around us. This brings awareness into the body, but it's also important how this awareness is held. The Buddha's way of teaching and training is through questioning and reflection. We're not trying to apply a catechism of, "The body is like this," repeating it over and over again. The awareness is an exploration, an investigation. We are asking ourselves, *What is the experience I'm having? Does it feel comfortable or not? Does it feel wholesome or not? Is this what mindfulness is, or not?* This kind of questioning is not an intellectual analysis, rather, we are trying to use contact as a mirror for reflecting and seeing more clearly.

We should, of course, reflect on the mind as well. *What's my mental state right now? What's the intention? What's the volition within the mind? Is this skillful or not skillful? How do I create and maintain a quality of skillfulness?* This is the kind of investigation we can carry with us throughout the day. Whether we are sitting in the Dhamma Hall, back at our *kuṭis*, or doing our chores, reflecting in this way internalizes our experience. It gives us an anchor for recognizing whether we're on track or not, whether we're according with Dhamma or have lost the plot.

We need to develop these essential skills so that they permeate every aspect of our practice, no matter where we are or what we are doing. As Ajahn Chah and so many other teachers have often said, "The Dhamma of the Buddha is everywhere." We don't have to go to the Pāli Canon to find it. We don't have to be sitting in a monastery to find it. It's the ability we have to recognize and see the truth, to see the way things truly are. It's everywhere. We can connect with it, we can contact it, and we can experience it.

The Kamma of Listening

Ajahn Yatiko • July 2013

Offering a morning reflection like this is a bit like planting a seed. What is said needs to be listened to with attention, care, and an open mind. When that happens, the seed has been planted in good soil. If the mind is not attentive or mindful, if it's off dreaming or thinking, then it gets no benefit from the reflection. But if the mind is attentive, focused, and keen to extract value, then even if what is said is very mundane or something we have heard a thousand times before, the mind can still benefit greatly. If we hear a reflection with the right attitude and a desire for what is wholesome, then value can be acquired even if we're not aware of it.

One of Ajahn Geoff's books is called *The Karma of Questions*. That's a fascinating theme to reflect on: What kind of kamma is involved in asking questions? It's not so much in getting an answer, but in asking the question that we create our kamma. Similarly, we can reflect on the kamma that is generated by listening to Dhamma. What does it mean to listen to Dhamma? Why is listening to Dhamma such profoundly good kamma? It's helpful to contemplate the value of listening to reflections and to appreciate receiving reflections even though it may sometimes feel as if we just want to get the experience over with as quickly as possible. If we listen attentively to Dhamma, we can realize insight right at that moment of listening, but also, days or even years later this Dhamma can give rise to wholesome thoughts, perceptions, and attitudes, planted like seeds in our minds. We never know when our listening to Dhamma—that initial seed—will bear fruit, but the quality of our listening will ensure the seed is in good soil.

Supporting Defilements or Supporting Dhamma

Luang Por Pasanno • June 2012

In yesterday's reading, Ajahn Baen emphasized a question that is quite commonly asked in the Forest Tradition. It's a very simple question that we should consider and contemplate in our practice: *Am I supporting the defilements, or am I supporting the development of Dhamma?* That very simple contemplation is critical, because our preferences and biases don't tend to lead us to question in that way. We tend to have thoughts like, *What do I prefer? What do I want? What view do I think is right?* Does that support our defilements of greed, hatred, and delusion, or does it support Dhamma? That's a question we don't often ask ourselves. But we need to bring it up, not only when we're watching and investigating the mind during formal meditation, but also during our day-to-day activities.

What is Dhamma? It has many facets, but importantly, Dhamma is that which is aligned with the path leading to the cessation of suffering. That's the whole point of the Buddha's teachings—to give us the tools to free ourselves from discontent, dissatisfaction, and dissonance. When the mind or heart is dissonant, we can see that clearly as we become aligned with Dhamma. When the mind and heart are each in tune, we can feel that right away, reflecting to ourselves, *This feels peaceful. This feels clear. This brings happiness and well-being. This is the opposite of following my attachments and desires, which always leads to dissatisfaction.*

Again, it's important to frequently ask ourselves, *Is this supporting the defilements or is this supporting Dhamma?* We ask this about our actions and our speech. We ask, *How am I establishing mindfulness and inner cultivation?* This is how we develop the Dhamma in our hearts and relinquish the defilements of the mind.

So What Am I, Chopped Liver?

Ajahn Amaro • December 2008

A theme we explored on the Thanksgiving Retreat was "complaining and blaming." I thought it would be a useful theme because our culture tends toward complaint. *If I'm suffering, then the way to the end of suffering is to complain or blame. I'm suffering, therefore it's somebody else's fault. I've been treated unfairly. This isn't right. It shouldn't be this way.* This is powerful conditioning in our lives. I remember a *New Yorker* cartoon with a student asking a monk, "You say life is suffering, but isn't it also complaining?" It's useful to take a period of time to reflect on the unconscious or semiconscious way we react to the experience of suffering—to reflect on the urge to be critical, to be negative, to complain, or to find fault in ourselves or in the things around us. While reflecting like that, we can broaden our view by inquiring into the matter. *Why do I think I shouldn't have to experience this illness, this pain, this weather, this food, this person sitting next to me?*

Then we can broaden our view further by consciously evoking a sense of appreciation and gratitude for the gifts and opportunities we have in our lives. This is a way to catch the mind's habitual movement toward criticism or complaint, its movement toward the classic glass-is-half-empty attitude. Evoking gratitude goes directly against that complaining, criticizing, blaming mind. But we need to make sure that this gratitude isn't based on a "think-pink" attitude—trying to sugarcoat things and pretend that we're not really feeling critical or negative. It doesn't help much to paste an artificial expression of gratitude on top of a negative mood or a feeling.

We begin with listening to the critical, blaming, or complaining mind, and hearing what that mind is saying. What's it coming up with? Is it the feeling of being unfairly treated, slighted, left out, or ignored? Can we hear the mind's cry of righteous indignation, *So what am I, chopped liver?* We receptively listen to the affronted, hurt, wounded, abandoned, irritated feelings, and hear the mind coming up with the reactions and thought processes that follow those feelings. We are simply allowing this experience to be known—this narrow, painful, reactionary state of complaining or feeling slighted. By bringing awareness to that, fully knowing its reactive quality, we can recognize and inquire, *This is a really painful state. Why would I choose to react like this? Why would I want to carry this around and burden my heart with this?* We're not saying to ourselves, *Oh, I'm supposed to be grateful now, I should plant some gratitude in here.* Instead we are simply seeing the painfulness of our narrow, self-centered reactions. Once we see this, then the very acknowledgment of that painfulness can enable us to let go and relax. In the broadening of our views and attitudes, what arises is gratitude. We are able to appreciate the bigger picture, the gifts and the lessons we have received, and the potential opportunities we have in the world.

Letting Go and Picking Up

Ajahn Karuṇadhammo • June 2013

Many of the practices we hear and read about in our tradition are focused on the process of letting go—how we let go of our habits and tendencies, as well as objects of mind. We do this to dwell in and experience the pure state of awareness that comes from not grasping or holding onto anything. This is the ultimate practice on the path: letting go of negative tendencies and realizing, at the end of the practice, a complete release, a complete letting go of everything, including the path that has taken us there.

I think it is also true that a substantial amount of the practice—if not all of the practice before completely letting go—also involves picking up. We learn this skill by discerning what it is we need to let go of and what it is we need to pick up and engage with. All the obstructions and hindrances to meditation—negative thoughts, reactions out of anger, greed, or confusion—are habits we can mindfully see arise in our minds and let go of to the best of our abilities.

In the same process so much of the path is involved with skillfully picking up different positive qualities—the habits of generosity, renunciation, energy, patience, truthfulness, determination, the practices of virtue, the sublime states of mind: loving-kindness, compassion, sympathetic joy, equanimity. All of these are using an object that we are picking up, and at least temporarily, holding onto. Our learning consists of understanding which different types of mind states we can access, which ones we want to let go of, and which ones we want to develop further. Letting go and picking up often go hand-in-hand so that as we begin to recognize a difficult mind state, such as anger arising, we realize it's something we want to let go of while at the same time—even simultaneously—we recognize something like patient endurance that needs to be picked up. For example, if a difficult situation arises, such as when a challenging person comes into our life, we can let go as we recognize the tendency to react out of anger while at the same time, we can pick up, develop, and nurture patience, the determination not to react, and kindness for the other person and for ourselves.

This morning I noticed one of the people in the meditation hall gently removing a spider from the room. How many people in the world will go to great pains to take a spider out of a room and set it free? Most of the time it's a quick stomping of the foot and that's it. This is something to pick up on, this type of sensitivity and caring for even the smallest of creatures. We can think of it as picking up a skillful mind habit. All of these actions have an impact on the mind and the heart. In our daily lives, we can explore what it is that's helpful for us to pick up, nurture and engage with, as well as what habits we can develop that will support us in our practice.

Enjoying That Enough-ness

Luang Por Pasanno • June 2012

It's beneficial for our practice to pay attention to how we use the four requisites—robe cloth, food, shelter, and medicine—and reflect on how we rely on people's generosity and kindness when we receive these offerings. Inner qualities that arise from reflecting in this way are contentment and gratitude, which are said to be a source of the highest blessings—*maṅgala*. These blessings are not only beneficial for us, but beneficial for others as well. People become inspired and confident when they see we are using the requisites in a wholesome way.

While reading Paul Breiter's book, *One Monk, Many Masters*, I was reminded of Ajahn Chah saying, "I have never seen any rich people in the world. I see a lot of people, a lot of visitors, but I've never seen any rich people in the world. All I've seen is people who don't have enough." That's a powerful reflection for us. No matter what the external conditions of abundance are, it doesn't actually mean one is rich or wealthy, because true wealth is not measured by the material goods one accumulates. The richness of one's life—having true wealth within the limits of the human condition—comes from having the ability to be happy and peaceful within those conditions.

We are learning to find satisfaction with the qualities of contentment and gratitude, rather than constantly seeking something more, something different, or something other than what we have. That's the way the mind usually works. The untrained mind is constantly seeking something else, whether it's in the material realm, in the realm of views and opinions, or even in the realm of meditative states. It's constantly looking for something else, not content with what it has or what it's experiencing. The problem with the human condition is this constant seeking and, of course, not really finding. So we need to learn how to be someone who has enough and to be someone who enjoys that "enough-ness."

The Mood Is Not Who You Are

Ajahn Yatiko • April 2012

There's always a mood present in our experience. It's amazing to think how the presence of a mood so completely shapes and conditions both our attitude and the way we see things. It's important to have straight vision—some sense of what our life is about, what it's for, and what it is we aspire to. This vision or aspiration provides a compass when moods arise that tear us apart and sometimes throw us into turmoil, irritability, anger, depression, or frustration. Various moods and emotions, often conditioned by relatively minor events, can arise and push us in a direction that's quite different than the major direction of our vision, our life, what we actually trust and what makes sense to us.

One of the lay residents here at Abhayagiri once talked about an interesting juxtaposition. One day, while feeling irritable, he came down from the mountain and went into the kitchen. There was a guest there who didn't seem to be pulling his weight, which affected this resident's mood. Later on that day, he got word that this guest was struggling to digest the news that his brother had been shot and killed. Juxtaposing reality and perception—the guest's shock and the resident's irritation, for instance—can put things into perspective and reveal how petty we can be.

It's human to get irritated when things aren't going as smoothly as we'd like or when we're feeling misunderstood.

But we need to recognize that indulging in such moods puts our present and future well-being at risk. We have this life and it's not a game. If we let our moods take control and spur us to act on impulse, then we wind up doing things that can damage our long-term interests and the well-being of others.

So when these unwelcome moods arise, it's important to do everything we can to gain perspective on them and remember that they come and go. We shouldn't blindly delight in good moods either. It's okay to enjoy a good mood, but if we get lost in it then we'll get lost when a bad mood comes around as well. There's no way around that. We can't realistically say, *I'll take the good moods and forget the bad moods.* We train ourselves in meditation with any mood that comes up. We take stock of it and remember that the mood is not who we are. When a mood arises, we do our best to recognize its existence and then investigate how it may be pushing us to act in ways that aren't helpful to our welfare or the welfare of others.

Putting the Four Noble Truths Into Action

Luang Por Pasanno • April 2013

As we bring the practice into our daily lives, it's immensely beneficial to use the Four Noble Truths when viewing experience—in our formal meditation, interactions with others, and engagements with various duties. This is not something to save for later—after studying the suttas, developing all the states of concentration and the psychic powers, we finally contemplate the Noble Truths and become enlightened—it's not like that. The Four Noble Truths are to be put into practice right now.

To do this, we need to establish a habit of reflecting and investigating in a particular way. First, by examining phenomena carefully—the quality of experience, and the results that come from interacting with experience in the usual way—we find there's always some kind of *dukkha*, some kind of suffering, stress, or discontent. Then we reflect on that, investigating its cause and how to bring about its cessation. When applying these steps, we're not viewing the world through the lens of self, of me and my problems, me and my accomplishments, me and my preferences, me and my views and opinions. We're looking instead from the perspective of dukkha, its cause, its cessation, and the path leading to its cessation. When we view experience like that, life becomes very simple and straightforward.

So we lift up that perspective in the mind and practice with it. We're not waiting patiently for some intuitive insight to arise spontaneously. We need to deliberately train the mind by frequently redirecting our attention and reflecting on experience in that way.

The Buddha gives us the practice method of using the Four Noble Truths as a lens to depersonalize experience. And when we use the right method, he says beneficial results are bound to follow. If we use the wrong method, however, our efforts will be futile. To illustrate these points, the Buddha offers some humorous similes. For example, he says that when we're wrongly seeking the fruits of practice, we're like a man seeking milk: knowing that milk comes from cows, he approaches a nursing cow, twists her horn, and then wonders why he doesn't get any milk. The reason, of course, is that he's using the wrong method. But if he were to use the right method by pulling on the cow's udder, then the milk would surely flow. In the same way, even if we understand the Four Noble Truths in principle, nothing significant will result if we keep those teachings in our heads as mere abstractions. That would be using the wrong method, because the most essential bit is missing: bringing the Noble Truths into our practice. On the other hand, when we do put them into practice and apply them skillfully—that is, when we use the right method—then we are bound to realize beneficial results.

Paying attention to the method and its application, putting it into practice, bringing the Four Noble Truths into our experience, reflecting upon and applying these truths—this is how we can reap the fruits of practice.

Doing What's Difficult to Do

Ajahn Ñāṇiko • July 2012

Living in a monastery can be very difficult—eating one meal a day, keeping precepts, trying to live and work together as a harmonious community. But as Master Hua said, "If we want to practice Dhamma, we have to do what's difficult to do, what others would not choose to do." Even though most people wouldn't choose to live in this way, there's an enormous benefit to what we're doing here. Living in community, we learn how to hold things lightly and take responsibility for what's happening in our minds.

During the work period, it's easy for one little event to trigger anger, irritation, or some sort of desire. If this happens when we're interacting with someone, the mind convinces us that it's the other person's fault, as if these defilements came from that other person. So it's good to remember that irritation, anger, and desires come from within our own minds. They arise there and then seek external objects to latch on to. That's why sometimes, no matter how easygoing we may be, when we come in contact with some little thing, we can become irritated—the conditions for that irritation were already there. And when we get stuck in irritation or anger with another community member, we can forget that it's *dukkha*. We're suffering and the other person is suffering too. Sometimes we can get angry at someone else because they're angry. This is ridiculous, but it's the way it works. The Buddha said, "If you don't react with anger to an angry person, then you win a battle hard to win." When interacting with others, we may need to swallow our pride from time to time, as difficult as that may be.

I remember during my third Rains Retreat in Thailand, I was doing walking meditation every day for several hours after the meal. There was a lot of doubt coming up. I was literally driving myself to tears with constant doubts in the mind. There I was on the walking meditation path, no one else was around, and I was mired in suffering because of this unstoppable mental proliferation. That's how it is sometimes. But these experiences are good to have—by going through them, we become stronger. Even so, it's difficult to do.

Master Hua said that we're aiming to develop a "long-enduring mind"—a mind that can sustain itself through the months and years without sinking far down, becoming dark, falling out of the robes, or not wanting to be in a monastery anymore. To develop this long-enduring mind, we need to come back to peace, to the skillful actions that help sustain us, and to the factors of letting go. We need to come back again and again, moment by moment. It may be difficult to do, but the reward is true freedom.

Responding to Wholesome Crowds

Luang Por Pasanno • April 2013

We are preparing for the annual *kaṭhina* ceremony today and visitors have already started arriving. In terms of our practice, everything that happens on occasions like this is merely sights, sounds, smells, tastes, touch, and mental objects. We tend to make a problem out of sense contact, but it's just that much, nothing more. Objectively speaking, what's taking place here? The day begins, there is a wave of people and activity that comes in—it arises. The day ends, the wave of people and activity goes out—it passes away. It's another arising and ceasing—an opportunity to pay attention to the way that things come and go.

Of course, there's more to deal with and manage today, because the number of visitors will be high. That's the reality of what's happening. But we don't need to get excited about it, create a story around it, worry about it, or try to get away from it. Rather, we can ask ourselves, *How am I holding all of this?* Are we able to return to mindfulness, over and over again? Do we have the ability to sustain a sense of clarity, discernment, kindness, and well-being? We can choose to let go of excitement, confusion, irritation, and aversion. Reactions like those are extra and completely unnecessary.

As a monastic community, we're solely dependent on the generosity of the lay community, and this is a time when that generosity is being vividly displayed. What can we offer as a gesture of appreciation for this generosity that gives us the ability to live our lives? It isn't through our getting swept up in excitement. It isn't through our shrinking away because of irritation. It's through our ability to hold a steadiness and clarity in our minds. Our ability to be clear and steady has a lot more value than the short-term satisfaction of allowing our minds to get swept up in our reactions. This ability is the basis for our practice, but also serves as a model for others. And that's what the world needs. It's a wonderful gift when people come to the monastery and see a model of wisdom operating in a group of people.

There are people coming—that's not an illusion. So help each other, pay attention to the situation, and look after what needs to be done. Be ready to respond with kindness and attentiveness to the people who arrive. Express your heartfelt appreciation. These people are here to offer support for the monastery. That kind of generosity is something to delight in with a sense of gratitude.

Being Willing to Make Mistakes

Ajahn Karuṇadhammo • May 2013

How much are we willing to learn from our mistakes? This is a crucial aspect of the training—the willingness to recognize when we've missed the mark as well as being open to making mistakes. It's not always easy to practice in this way. I think many of us here come with conditioning around how important it is to be right all the time. We can grow up with a sense of shame—*Unless I'm doing everything perfectly all the time, then something is wrong with me.* As far as I can tell, there are only a few lucky people who learned while growing up that it's just fine to make mistakes. In the community here, there are many of us who are strong-willed in certain ways. We have plenty of leaders here and sometimes it can be difficult for us to break that classic paradigm, *The way I think we should do it is the right way.*

We begin to unravel this paradigm by learning that it's okay to not be right all the time and to use honest self-appraisal to examine ourselves. This allows us to say *Okay, perhaps since everybody else is doing it a different way, I need to consider that, or a number of people are indicating to me that I may have missed the mark—maybe I should think carefully about what happened.* This is a sign of internal strength. I also believe highly realized people tend to take this approach as well. Those who have penetrated the perception of not-self can see there is no "me" or "myself" that needs defending. They know it's not a problem if they're not always right.

This comes down to a matter of skill. Either it's a skill we've learned, or one we haven't, or perhaps we've partially taken it on—but it's nothing personal. As Luang Por Pasanno was saying, even the Buddha after his enlightenment was constantly readjusting. Sometimes he'd set down rules, only to realize later they needed to be changed. In those cases he would call the monks together, explain the need to alter a rule, and adjust it accordingly. Right after his enlightenment, the Buddha was inclined not to teach. As the story goes, the Brahmā God Sahampati realized this was the Buddha's inclination, came down from the brahmā realm, appeared before the Buddha, and said, "Please reconsider this. There are those who can learn!" The Buddha thought, *Maybe there is a possibility of teaching others how to realize what I have realized.* So even at that point he readjusted, and he certainly didn't take it personally.

This is a good reflection to bring to mind. Essentially, it's a reminder to be honest with ourselves—whether it's relating to community life, the monastic discipline, the training, the views and opinions about how things should be done, or one's personal meditation practice—we can strive for a more open and balanced point of view. We do this by honestly looking at our internal experiences, allowing ourselves to be present with our fears of being wrong, and saying to ourselves, *Okay, I need to make a change; I need to adjust.* And then simply let it go and make the adjustment. Once that's done and the change has been made, we can move on and not worry about it so much.

A Foundation of
Love and Acceptance

Ajahn Yatiko • August 2013

In this community at Abhayagiri, we need to take care of each other. If we don't have a foundation of love and care for each other, then the foundation of our lives is on very shaky ground.

I have a tremendous amount of respect and affection for each person here, no matter what their personality traits may be. It is important, I believe, that we give each other the space needed to be who we are. We conform externally; we have these robes, shave our heads, and look similar. Yet we are all completely different individuals, remarkably so. We need to allow everybody to be who and what they are—to be themselves. We mustn't start from a position of being unable to accept something or someone. The starting point in practice is being able to accept other people and to accept ourselves.

With that as a foundation, we then work with the defilements. It is not as if we work with the defilements as a condition for accepting ourselves—*Once my defilements are under control, then I'll accept myself.* No. We start with acceptance, and from there we can work with whatever difficulties arise. Likewise, there's no need to expect other people to live up to our standards of monastery etiquette, harmony, or even our standards for being happy. It is okay to have a miserable day, to be gloomy for quite awhile. We are what we are, and we can accept each other whether we are happy, sad, anxious, excited, or afraid. That is a very good starting position on which we can build our practice.

Comfortable in Any Circumstance

Luang Por Pasanno • July 2013

It looks like it's going to be hot again today. Most of us are uncomfortable when it's hot like this. So what we need to do, as Dhamma practitioners, is learn how to adapt. We learn to dwell with mindfulness and equanimity whether things are to our liking or not. The tendency is to wait for conditions we like and when they arise, only then do we say to ourselves, *Okay, now I can practice.* It's an attitude that can easily become habitual. But being tied to the human condition as we are, it's rare for things to be just right. So what we need to do is develop a willingness to work with conditions as they are. If it's really hot, then we adjust our pace accordingly, perhaps we slow down what we're doing. We may say to ourselves, *Really, truly, I can't practice now. I have to wait for this to be over and then I can practice.* That's a common response, but we shouldn't waste our time with it.

Often we deal with imperfect conditions by getting in touch with our "inner complainer" that's whining away, going on and on about how miserable we feel. Instead of mindlessly doing that, we can use challenging circumstances as a means of investigating the habit of complaining. We do this by watching the mind trying to convince itself that physical discomfort automatically means we have to experience mental discomfort. When the mind is adopting that sort of misunderstanding and complaining about the circumstances, we observe how this simply perpetuates suffering. It's not that we're trying to sugar coat the tendency to complain by saying to ourselves, *Oh, isn't this wonderful? I just love it when it's 108 degrees outside.* Instead we're facing reality and being honest with ourselves. At the same time, we understand that simply because circumstances are less than ideal, they do not also have to be a source of complication or oppression.

The point is to distinguish between the direct, physical experience and the layers of mental complication we add to that experience. When we do that, it gives us an inner refuge, allowing us to be comfortable in any circumstance. That's one of the magical things about Dhamma practice. We can be at ease and clear in any circumstance if we're willing to direct our attention in a skillful way.

The Role of Observance Days

Ajahn Amaro • August 2008

The purpose of our weekly Observance Day is to put our usual daily tasks down and focus on the precepts and the formal spiritual qualities of our life. It's a day of recollecting and observing, of remembering the Dhamma and our original motivation for being here at the monastery. It's a time to remember the possibility we have as human beings to let go of all confusion, delusion, aversion, greed, and self-centeredness. It's a time for renewing our motivation and to begin again fresh.

As monastics, we shave our heads, taking the hair back to the root, back to the source, to begin again. There's that quality of tidying up—cleaning the shrine room, cleaning the kitchen, squaring things away, renewing our precepts. On a practical and symbolic level we're keeping the monastery tidy and looking after the things that have been offered for our use. On the internal level, we're remembering our priorities and helping to clarify the central principles of our lives.

The activities of the Observance Day—taking the precepts, shaving the head, having the all-night vigil, and putting aside the work routine—are all geared toward reinforcing the reason we're here at the monastery. We're not here to construct *kuṭis*, post pictures on the website, cook meals, or any of the 10,000 tasks that occupy our attention. The whole point of this place existing, this gathering of human beings on this particular patch of hillside, is to realize the Dhamma—to let go of greed, hatred, and delusion. That's the reason we're here. Our preparations for the Observance Day and the day itself are all meant to help us to remember, *Oh, right, that's what it's all for, of course. Why was I forgetting that?* That's the purpose of all the construction projects and committees. That's why we take care of these duties and keep the place clean and tidy. That's what it's for—the realization of Dhamma.

Blown Into Cosmic Dust

Luang Por Pasanno • April 2013

The Buddha encouraged us to contemplate aging, sickness, and death every single day. It's essential that we make an effort do that, because the mind's nature is to forget about these contemplations. It inclines away from them and instead, inclines toward thoughts of eternal youth and health. For the most part, death doesn't exist for us. So we have to make it conscious in our practice by realizing the limitations of the human condition on the physical level. We're bound to this body that's constantly aging. Even when we're young, it's still aging. The reason a baby gets born in the world is because it's too old to stay in the womb. That aging process continues on after birth.

This is a supportive reflection for us—it's not intended to make us miserable or depressed. It's intended to bring up wholesome mental states to counteract the mind's tendency toward *pamāda*—being careless and not very circumspect regarding the truths of our existence. The three recollections on aging, sickness, and death help establish a sense of heedfulness and spiritual urgency. We have this opportunity to hear the Dhamma, to study the Dhamma, to practice the Dhamma, to live a life in accord with the Dhamma. Reflecting on that makes us grateful for this opportunity to practice and that's vital, because it's easy to let the opportunity slip by.

We recollect the nature of the human body—that our lives are subject to aging, sickness, and death. For all of our seeming solidity, we're left to nature when we die—our bodies dissipate and disappear. The Buddha taught the charnel ground contemplations, which encourage us to examine the body's process of dissolution after death. It changes shape, bloats, disintegrates, and dries out until just the sinews and bones are left. The bones are then scattered until there's little remaining but a small pile of gray dust. Then a wind comes along and blows it here and there until there is nothing left. For all of our obsessions about ourselves—our worries, fears, and anxieties around health and physical well-being, and all the uncertainties in our lives—it is absolutely certain that, on a physical level, we're all going to be blown into cosmic dust.

Now when we contemplate that fact, it's not to be picked up in a nihilistic way, but rather with the sense of urgency that's needed to establish the heart with skillful spiritual qualities—the sense of urgency we need to keep attending to our actions of body, speech, and mind, so that they're conducive to clarity, wisdom, and wholesome states of mind.

We often recite the "Five Subjects for Frequent Recollection." When reciting the fifth, we recollect: "I'm the owner of my kamma, heir to my kamma, born of my kamma, related to my kamma, abide supported by my kamma. Whatever kamma I shall do, for good or for ill, of that I will be the heir." These recollections help us establish our kamma—our actions of body, speech, and mind—in what is wholesome, skillful, and beneficial, in what bears fruit in terms of peace and clarity, happiness and well-being. So it behooves us to take responsibility for these contemplations, to reflect upon them and develop them in our practice.

When Generosity Motivates
Our Practice

Ajahn Yatiko • April 2013

This morning in meditation I was reflecting on the various offerings that have been made to me in my life. It's a really wonderful exercise to do from time to time. This sitting cloth was made by Ajahn Ñāṇiko. I'm wearing clothes that Dennis gave me. David's mother, Ayya Santussika, gave the monastery this vibrating alarm clock. Ajahn Jotipālo made this wooden holder for the bell. Ajahn Saññamo gave me the socks I'm wearing, which were given to him by Tan Khemako, who received them from a layperson. The flowers on the shrine came from our friend Apple.

As monastics, it's nice that we can name the specific person who has offered almost any material item around us. By doing this we realize that absolutely everything we have is a gift from faithful and generous people. As alms mendicants, we rely on the faithful generosity of the laity to provide us with food as well as other material supports—robe cloth, shelter, and medicine. Our survival is sustained through the gifts of others. When we reflect on this, quite naturally the result is a sense of gratitude and appreciation.

At the same time, such generosity and support can cause us to ask, *Why am I allowing myself to receive all this goodness and kindness?* The reason is that having faith in the Buddha's teachings, we became intent upon being free from greed, hatred, and delusion, and so we came here to devote ourselves to the Buddha's path—a path which takes a great deal of commitment and effort. This is why we receive so much goodness from others, which in turn inspires us to practice well.

However, this dynamic can create a problem. Many of us come from a strongly guilt-driven culture, and we can say things to ourselves like, *Everyone is supporting me, so I should practice hard, I should do sitting meditation and walking meditation. I should learn the suttas.* For us, the word *should* can mean that if we don't do it, we're really bad monks. That's the completely wrong approach. Instead, we can reflect that, *Since everything is given to me, even this body doesn't belong to me. It belongs to the faithful—it's merely loaned to me by them.* With that in mind, there's still the sense that we *should* practice, but it comes from a completely different "should." It's more like a voluntary "should." It comes from a wholesome desire to practice because we know that it's worthwhile, a decent thing to do. We come to realize, *It's for my own benefit as well as for the benefit of others.*

As we walk on the meditation path, we can contemplate the significant difference between the "should" of guilt and the "should" of the natural and wonderful activity we're interested in doing. We can reflect on the blessings of our lives, the things that have come to us, and realize what a wonderful opportunity we have to practice and cultivate the path of the Buddha.

Applying a Wholesome Attitude

Luang Por Pasanno • May 2012

Yesterday Ajahn Saññamo gave us a reading about sweeping leaves—how sweeping can be an integral part of our practice. His reading came from a book detailing the practices at Ajahn Baen's monastery. It is a big monastery with large open areas, so every day, everyone goes out to sweep. In his monastery, sweeping is part of the practice and training. That's the way it should be for us as well—and not only with sweeping. All the various chores, duties, and responsibilities we have are part of the training. They're not simply things to fill the time, or excuses to take a break from practice to get something "practical" done. Rather, they allow us to examine the attitudes we bring to the activities we perform and to evaluate the way we spend our time.

How *do* we spend our time? Do we spend it thinking about ourselves, and resenting anything that impinges on our preferences, views, and opinions of how we imagine things should be? Or do we spend our time engaged in what we do with generosity and kindness, with a sense of relinquishment? Do we put energy and effort into our chores and duties, or do we try to slide by, thinking to ourselves, *If people see me moving around the place, maybe they won't notice that I'm not really getting much done.* These are some of the attitudes we might bring to our practice. It's helpful to skillfully engage with these attitudes, because they can give rise to unwelcome, problematic moods.

Once a mood like that does arise—if we're engaged with what's going on—we can respond with an energetic attitude, asking ourselves, *How can I shift this mood in a positive way?*

There's a story Ajahn Sumedho tells about sweeping during his early days at Wat Pah Pong. It is a standard practice in forest monasteries to sweep the grounds, and Wat Pah Pong is no different. The day before each Observance Day, the bell would ring to indicate that it was time for sweeping, and all the monks were supposed to go out and sweep the large, dusty central areas of the monastery. Ajahn Sumedho relates how he didn't like going out into the heat and the dust, nor did he like the activity of group sweeping, so he'd usually wait to join the group until he was about the last person to come out. Because he took so long to join the group, he'd often get the last broom, which was usually some scruffy old thing, made of a few little twigs that didn't really do much. Ajahn Sumedho said he would go along and scratch a bit at the ground, stand, wait, internally grumble and complain, and say to himself, *This is really stupid. I don't like this. Why do we have to do this?* His mind would go on and on. Of course, Ajahn Chah noticed what was happening, and one day during the sweeping period he walked past Ajahn Sumedho and said, "Wat Pah Pong—is it suffering?" Ajahn Sumedho reflected on this, *Wat Pah Pong—is it suffering? No, of course not! Wat Pah Pong isn't suffering! It's me! It's not Wat Pah Pong. I like Wat Pah Pong. I'm the one making suffering out of this. It's me.* That was a powerful and significant insight for him—to see that the external situation is one thing, and whether or not he adds suffering to it is another. After that, Ajahn Sumedho put more energy and enthusiasm into the sweeping. By doing so and reflecting, he decreased the suffering for himself and turned sweeping into an enjoyable experience.

We can use our chores in the same way—to bring up energy, a sense of relinquishment, generosity, service, and mindfulness. Doing that helps to provide continuity for our practice; it keeps us reflecting on what's happening in the mind, what's going on with our attitudes and perspectives. We can see more clearly the story the mind is telling us, so we learn how to work with it in a skillful way. Sometimes it's easy to focus on getting a particular chore over with, so we can go back to our dwellings and do "our practice." In doing this, we forget that our mental state and what's going on in the mind *is* our practice.

Not Taking Refuge in the Weather

Ajahn Jotipālo • December 2012

On mornings like this—when it's pouring down with rain, when it's not comfortably warm, and we have been assigned a wet and inconvenient job working outside—in this situation, the mind may rebel or complain.

It was quite a cold morning and pouring down rain during the first work meeting I attended at Abhayagiri. Everybody was going to be working outside because of last-minute preparations for the winter retreat. Before the work began we were gathered together listening to Ajahn Pasanno's morning reflection. The mood in the room was pretty glum when Ajahn said to us, "Well, it's a good thing we don't take refuge in the weather." When he said that, my mood immediately changed. We were only going to get wet, that's all. We had places to dry our clothes and we would be outside for only a couple hours. In addition, it was going to be really good work, a substantial service to the monastery.

Ajahn Pasanno's comment has stuck with me over time, and encouraged me to ask myself, *What am I taking refuge in? Is it the work I'm doing? The relationships I'm cultivating? Am I taking refuge in wanting to feel good and not being inconvenienced in body or mind?* After reflecting like that it can be easy to set aside my aversion to rain. On days when there are tasks I don't want to do, I can look at my perceptions and ask myself, *What am I taking refuge in? What assumptions am I making? How can I see this situation from a different perspective so that I might incline my mind toward a brighter state?* When I reflect in this way, the work period or the task I'm attending to can be quite enjoyable.

Krueng Yoo: The Tool
That Sustains Us

Ajahn Yatiko • July 2012

It is worth reflecting on the Thai phrase *krueng yoo*. *Krueng* literally means tool. When it is combined with *yoo*, the loose translation is a tool used to sustain. With Dhamma in mind, krueng yoo can mean a practice that is used to help sustain one's spiritual existence. So we might reflect and ask ourselves, *In my daily life, what do I use to occupy my time? What is the practice that sustains me?*

At times we may say to ourselves, *I've been scattered lately, and I really want to focus more.* So we make a determination, *I'm going to be more focused in what I do.* That can be a pitfall if our resolve comes from the standpoint that our situation is not acceptable or from a desire to control or coerce, rather than the standpoint of taking an interest in examining our experience. It's like parents who constantly tell their child what to do, trying to force the child to act in certain ways. After a while, the child doesn't bother listening. The child and parents can end up with a split. It can be the same with our minds—we can have this split as well. We might try to force ourselves to focus or practice harder, but there's a part of the mind that can rebel, that doesn't want to do be forced.

Rather than trying to force the mind, we can ask ourselves, *Why is it that I don't want to practice sometimes? What is that about?*

Without forcing and imposing our control, we can get to the root of the problem through skillful investigation. Instead of *telling*, we're *asking*—we're probing, inquiring, and looking for the defilements that lurk within. Forcing ourselves to do something doesn't actually deal with any of the defilements. We need to investigate: What are the conditions that give rise to the defilements? What causes them to hang around? This gives rise to an understanding of ourselves and an understanding of suffering. We might say that investigating in this way is our krueng yoo.

When Help Is Needed

Luang Por Pasanno • August 2012

One focus of our practice is to look after each other and help each other out. In one discourse where the Buddha finds Venerable Anuruddha and his friends living in the forest, we see that they are intent on formal practice, but whenever something needs to be done, they come out of meditation and help each other. That is a very beautiful story from the suttas. Our tendency, however, is to try doing everything by ourselves, which is usually not so comfortable. But when we learn to help each other, it's much more convenient for everyone. It's like the convenience of using two hands to wash. When one hand is trying to wash itself, the job takes quite a while and is less than thorough. But with two hands washing each other, it's quicker and everything gets clean.

Similarly, as human beings living together with duties and chores, we can learn to look out for the many ways we can help one another. A lot of this practice comes from the cultivation of mindfulness, of paying attention. It's so easy to have our blinders on and think, *I'm only doing this task, this is what I'm doing.* We don't have enough attention and clear comprehension to reflect and ask ourselves, *What are other people doing? Do they need assistance? Is there some way I can help out?*

When we reflect like this for the sake of others, it helps us cultivate mindfulness. It is also a way we can step outside of ourselves. So often we set boundaries—me and my autonomous self. While this can have a useful function, it can also be quite limiting and isolating, and sometimes leads to selfish behavior. What we are doing instead is learning how to let go of the fixation on "I, me, and mine"—to relinquish that self-centric modality of living in the world. This fixation, the Buddha said, is one of the main sources of *dukkha*. By looking out to see how we can be of assistance to others, we undermine that modality and give ourselves the opportunity to experience well-being.

Christmas Day:
A Bodhisatta of Compassion

Ajahn Karuṇadhammo • December 2012

It's Christmas day. I don't know much about Christianity. Even though I grew up as a Christian, I wasn't very attentive to the religion. As Buddhists, we can sometimes have our own limited perspectives about Christianity. We may find ourselves making different judgments about the religion, or at least about how it's practiced in the world these days. But one of the more positive memories that I have from growing up as a Christian is Christ's essential message of compassion. Very similar to the Buddhist motivation for compassion, Christ expressed his wish for others to be free from suffering. We find compassion inherent within the Four Noble Truths—we're looking at the truth of suffering and how to end it.

One of the messages I remember from my early Christian upbringing was that Christ was there to help others find an end to suffering. As the teachings from Christianity suggest, Christ was so tuned into the suffering of others and had so much compassion for wanting to end it that he offered his life on the cross for all other beings, saying that he would willingly die so that others could be absolved of their sins. That's not something that we as Buddhists think is possible—that we could take somebody else's kamma away from them. But the notion of wanting to be able to do that, even if it's not possible, is quite a powerful contemplation. The sense of wanting others to be free of suffering so much that we are willing to die for it—that's, at least, in the Buddhist paradigm, the sign of a real Bodhisatta.

Whatever the reality is, having that kind of aspiration—of wishing to be free from suffering and wishing to help others do the same—is a useful message. As followers of the Buddha, we aim to figure out how we can realize that. It means focusing our attention on the First Noble Truth and recognizing the need to penetrate it. Before we can try to help others become truly liberated from their suffering, we have to face it within our own lives. We have to be willing to take a close look at this *dukkha*—to experience and know what it really means before we can move on to understanding its origin, letting it go, and developing the path. This entails honest self-appraisal, and it starts right at home inside ourselves. We begin to open up to this Noble Truth because we are willing to look at our own unskillful habits and the unwholesome ways that we've learned to operate in the world.

For all of us, deep conditioning in some way or another causes us to continue our old habits of behavior, which tend to bring on more difficulty and stress. This includes the way we view experience or view other people and what we try to get from the world or from our relationships with other people—the whole gamut of what it is that we do in our attempts to gain happiness and gratification. It takes bravery to go deep inside, look at the cause of suffering in our lives, have compassion for that, and begin the process of uprooting it. This requires honesty and integrity to truly look at ourselves. As we do that, we naturally experience more sensitivity, knowing that this same process is happening to everyone else too.

Because we are willing to examine ourselves and understand our own suffering, this helps us to see that others are experiencing the same difficulties as us. We can be more accepting of other's foibles and bad habits because we realize that all of us make these same mistakes when we try and take care of our own needs. If we have compassion for ourselves, then we can have compassion for everybody else. To me, that seems like a way we can understand and emulate some of the teachings that come from the Christian traditions.

Death and the Nature of Waves

Ajahn Amaro • November 2008

We received news yesterday from Koṇḍañña's partner that he's fading rapidly. He's in a hospice in San Francisco. Jay passed away a few days ago. Ajahn Karuṇadhammo is having surgery today. While we were sitting this morning after doing the *paritta* chanting for Ajahn Karuṇadhammo and Koṇḍañña, an image came to mind of different waves coming in from the ocean and moving toward the shore. There's the wave named Jay, having reached the shore and broken up, and the Koṇḍañña wave, a wave moving steadily toward the shore. Similarly, with Ajahn Karuṇadhammo and all the rest of us, there are these little waves on the great ocean of nature, steadily, inexorably moving toward the shore. They sustain a form for a particular time—what we call Jay or whatever—they move along picking up material, and finally reach the shore and disperse. These energy waves flow through the oceans of the world. When they reach the beach, there's the sound of the waves crashing on the shore, and then the energy disperses.

When we reflect on the imminence of death, it seems like such a dramatic thing—a life coming to an end. It seems so personal. The Amaro wave seems so different from the Pasanno wave, the Cunda wave, the Ṭhitapañño wave. They all seem separate and different. But when we look at them from a broader perspective, it's merely the same ocean of stuff, with different patterns of energy moving through it. The waves have a certain coherence, a certain individuality that's apparent, but there's no need to get excited about this wave versus that wave, to worry about which one is closer to the shore, or to think that anything desperately bad has happened when a wave reaches the shore. It's simply what waves do. That's their ultimate destination, their nature. Their energy disperses.

Sickness and death are very much in our consciousness these days. Ajahn Karuṇadhammo going under the knife, Ajahn Toon passing away, Jay passing away, and Koṇḍañña in his last days. So this is a good time to cultivate a sense of knowing the nature of waves, and to look upon our own lives and the lives of others with the same kind of equanimity and evenness. We're simply watching the ocean doing its thing. Waves forming, flowing in, breaking on the shore, washing out. That's it, no big deal.

We can also reflect on the distinctions between our lives and the lives of others, those we know and those we don't know. We can see how different textures of feeling can gather around particular waves. They seem so important because there's a name for each wave, the name of someone close to us. But the knowing quality within us reflects that it's just another wave. How could it be so different or special even when it has our own name on it? This body, these aches and pains, these ailments, this lifespan—there's that knowing within us which can realize, *Well, it's not such a big deal. Waves rise up, they move, they break. That's it, no big thing.* We have the ability to discover that quality of evenness, steadiness, and balance. We can have an unshakable and profoundly stable equanimity which is undisturbed in the midst of all that arises, moves toward the shore, and disperses.

Joy: Rising Up and Going Forth

Ajahn Yatiko • May 2012

I was speaking with somebody recently who shared that he was finding it difficult to settle into the joy of life, to sit back and enjoy being alive. He thought that something was wrong with that. I explained to him that from a Buddhist perspective it's not about settling into a joy that's supposedly inherent in life, rather, joy is something that comes from past action, from kamma. As my father used to say, "There's no such thing as a free lunch." That's so true and a good reflection for the practice. If we want to experience joy, it takes effort. How could it be any other way? While it may seem somewhat paradoxical, the effort needed for joy to arise must be directed toward letting go.

Now I have fairly passive tendencies and so for me, letting go requires making an effort to counteract those tendencies. So letting go is not a passive experience, but an experience of going forth, as if I have to rise up and go forth into the present moment. It's a wonderful relief when I do this—it's joyful. On the other hand, for people who tend to be driven and goal-oriented, the process of letting go is very different. For them, letting go comes with the realization that they don't need to put forth a self-motivated, Herculean, obsessive effort. It still takes effort, but for them the effort mostly goes toward relaxing and calming the driven quality of their energy.

Once a sense of joy arises, it takes more effort to keep it going. We get onto our walking paths, walk, put forth effort, and, when the mind wanders and moves away from its center of awareness, we bring it back. At some point joy may arise. It's wonderful when that happens, but how long does that joy last? The image that comes to mind is one of those carnival wheels that spins around for about thirty seconds, then slows down, and finally stops. That's akin to the arising of joy and the way joy can be sustained. We put in effort—spinning the wheel—and from that effort joy arises. Then the wheel stops, and we exert our effort again. Over time, with our continued effort, we can keep the wheel spinning longer, and joy sustains itself longer.

When it comes to making our walking and sitting practice sustainable, we do have to enjoy it. We can turn our attention to that joy. Right now the weather is beautiful, the sun is out and it's filtering through the trees as we walk or sit in the forest. It's quiet, peaceful, and easy to enjoy this opportunity to put forth effort toward something that's absolutely blameless and wholesome. It's a remarkable opportunity. If we can enjoy it, cultivate a sensitivity for the beauty, and develop the wonderful experience of being free and unburdened, then that's going to be a great help to our practice, our monastic lives, and our spiritual journey.

Mindfulness With
Clarity and Discernment

Luang Por Pasanno • August 2012

Yesterday at teatime, we were talking about *sampajañña*, clear comprehension, which is a quality we can reflect on in our daily practice. When the Buddha speaks about mindfulness—*sati*—he rarely treats mindfulness as an isolated quality. It's usually in conjunction with some other quality—particularly, clear comprehension, *sati-sampajañña*. Without clear comprehension, our mindfulness tends to be rather narrowly focused. We can forget that the Buddha is encouraging us to have a broadness of attention and awareness and a reflective quality while we are cultivating mindfulness. So we need to make clear comprehension an integral part of our cultivation and development of mindfulness.

Clear comprehension has different functions, duties, and purposes. There is clear comprehension of the object of our attention, but there are many other aspects as well. For instance, the sense of being free of delusion is one example of sampajañña operating within the mind. With non-delusion we have a sense of clearly comprehending our biases or lack of biases and refraining from bringing a self-position into our experiences.

We can also clearly comprehend how to practice in a way that's in keeping with whatever time and place we happen to be in. Ajahn Chah used to give a classic example of this having to do with a senior monk who would visit him at his monastery. In the morning they would go on alms round together into one of the villages around Wat Pah Pong. Ajahn Chah said that this was often a source of slight irritation because although this monk was very mindful, he didn't clearly comprehend the situation. As the visiting monk would lead a group on alms round, he would mindfully walk toward a buffalo pen, because he didn't notice that he wasn't walking on the road anymore. Or while he was being very focused, he would fail to recognize that he was walking on the left side of the road and all of the villagers were waiting off to the right side of the road. He would mindfully walk past them and start heading off into the paddy fields. Ajahn Chah would say, "Go right, go right," or "Go left, go left." Mindfulness requires clear comprehension so that we are aware of the appropriate time and place in each circumstance.

Another aspect of clear comprehension pertains to the different personalities and temperaments people have. Different people need attending to in different ways, and we need to adjust our actions and attitudes accordingly. Otherwise we may offend, upset, or miscommunicate with the people around us. Clear comprehension allows us to see how to choose the best response for each person we interact with.

In the Visuddhimagga, Ācariya Buddhaghosa suggests that sampajañña is a synonym for discernment; specifically, it's the discernment we use to determine what Dhamma to apply, depending on the situation we're in and the experience that's arising for us.

As we go about our day, we use reflective awareness to get the best sense of how to apply sati-sampajañña. We do not need to apply mindfulness and clear comprehension in a mechanical way. When we do our daily chanting, we recollect the qualities of the Dhamma, and one of these qualities is *opanayiko*: leading inward. The function of our practice is to draw our attention inward; to draw the world and interaction with the world around us, inward. That is how we are able to hold things with clarity and discernment, applying sati-sampajañña to see the Dhamma clearly.

Eye of the Hurricane

Ajahn Karuṇadhammo • November 2013

We have a full community once again. With all of the comings and goings, right now there seems to be a confluence of
comings—everybody is present within the community for at
least a little while. We also have a fairly sizable group of long-
term residents, visitors, and guests—more people than we've
been accustomed to in the past few weeks. Notice the effect of
that. Try to keep in mind the sense of being in a community
and learning from all the experiences of living with and relating to different people. We work together, make decisions, offer suggestions, receive suggestions, and experience the whole
interplay of human interaction. We can reflect on how to do
this skillfully and remember the importance of staying centered while in activity, trying not to let the senses be pulled
out in different directions. It helps to take a moment and come
back to the center of awareness in the body.

Many of us sometimes have a fantasy of being in total solitude and not having to interact with other people. I know I sure
do. Or we imagine living in a small community with only one or
two other people. However, one of the advantages of living and
working together in a sizable community with a fair amount of
engagement is the quality of learning that takes place and the
understanding we develop when we stay in the center of awareness without being pulled out into many different directions.
It's like being in the eye of a hurricane where there are very

strong winds around us—winds that could cause anxiety, fear, disturbance, or agitation. But right in the middle of the storm is the eye where it is very calm and still. We can place ourselves in that center so that we are alert and aware, where our senses are restrained and not moving out. Within this center, there is a receptivity to what's going on so that we are not totally isolated from the environment. We can respond appropriately, but the attention stays focused, particularly on the body. The body is the best place for maintaining that sense of presence. As we move through the day we can try to stay in the eye of the hurricane.

Practicing What Works

Luang Por Pasanno • August 2013

When we reflect on the best way to practice, it's good to focus on what works for us. We may read about various techniques and methods and wonder which is the right one for us. We can ask ourselves, *What have I done that works? What has helped the mind relinquish its attachments and defilements? What has helped the mind become more peaceful, settled, and clear?*

As we practice, we come to realize what works for us will change, depending on conditions. Simply because something worked today doesn't mean it's going to work tomorrow, and what didn't work in the past may work for us now. This makes it necessary to adapt and experiment. Ajahn Chah used to repeat a quote from one of his teachers, Ajahn Tong Rat, who taught that the practice is very straightforward and easy: "If the defilements come high, then duck; if they come low, then jump." Within the bounds of *sīla*, morality, we practice with whatever the situation demands—whatever works—as long as it has a wholesome outcome. This entails asking ourselves, *How might I work with this particular situation?* Once we have a sense of what might be a proper approach, we put it into practice and evaluate the results.

This points to an ongoing, evolving relationship between how we practice and how the mind works within this practice. It takes time to discover skillful ways of engaging with that relationship. It's a learning process. But by sticking with this process, by taking a genuine interest in it, we can develop a good sense of what practices are truly beneficial—what truly works for us.

Two Kinds of Fools

Ajahn Yatiko • July 2013

One of the things Ajahn Chah taught was what he called "earthworm wisdom." For many people, earthworms aren't worth appreciating. But it's earthworms that till the soil, and if they weren't continually working away, the soil would be infertile and incapable of supporting growth. That's a nice reflection, something to chew on.

The higher aspects of the teachings are certainly worth reflecting on, and there is a lot of profundity to penetrate. But it's also true that we live in a community and very often, community living is where the rubber hits the road. This is where we have contact, where we come together and rub up against our rough edges. Everyone in the community has the potential to make mistakes and cause offense or harm. When a mistake happens it can trigger different responses, both from the one who made the mistake, and from the one receiving the consequences of that mistake. In particular, the Buddha says, there are two kinds of fools in the world. One is a fool who, when having made a mistake—either an offense or a hurtful action toward another person—doesn't ask for forgiveness. The other kind of fool is one who when asked for forgiveness, refuses to give it. Do we sometimes act like one of those fools? That's something else to reflect upon.

We live in this community and hope that it is a wise community. We want to establish, maintain, and care for harmony here, because it is valuable and also because it is vulnerable. Like all relationships, those we have with our companions here require our generosity, and we have to put our hearts into that. We do this by opening our eyes, taking a look around, seeing how people are doing, and responding with our hearts. We reach out to people who look like they may be struggling, not doing so well, or needing a little bit of a lift. And in our hearts we forgive those who've made mistakes, whether they've asked for forgiveness or not. That's just ordinary kindness, but it's earthworm kindness—it's what creates an environment in the community that is very beautiful and uplifting. It provides the tilled soil from which fertility, growth, and development of individuals can take place.

Solitude in our practice is important in helping us to relinquish the unskillful views we've picked up in the past from misguided teachers, friends, books, and other unhelpful sources—views that have influenced us in ways not easily recognized. We need solitary practice to clearly see those views and the effects of our prior conditioning—to discern the Buddha-Dhamma for ourselves. But we have to be careful that our solitary practice doesn't create a type of selfishness or self-centered point of view. Living in community helps us remember to open our eyes and see that there are people here who are going through the same difficulties we are, and who may need the same sort of support we have received. It is helpful to be conscious of that, expand our vision, and care for the people around us. We are like earthworms tilling the spiritual soil of the community so it is a fertile place for growth in the Dhamma. When we come from a place of generosity and care, there can be a strong feeling that we are living under very special circumstances. This in turn uplifts our solitary practice and encourages a more en-compassing perspective.

A Day Worthy of Veneration

Luang Por Pasanno • June 2011

This evening is the night of our Lunar Observance. It's an opportunity to recollect the refuges and precepts, and to reflect on the direction of our spiritual practice and whether or not we need this direction to change. In the Thai language, the Observance Day is called *Wan Phra* which is roughly translated as *Holy Day*, *Monk Day*, or perhaps *Day Worthy of Veneration*.

As Ajahn Chah used to say, the Buddha made these special days part of our training, and it's not too much for the Buddha to have asked that we observe them—to have regular days worthy of veneration. We do it once a week. Over a month, we get four days worthy of veneration and twenty-six ordinary days, which is a good balance. The problem is we sometimes treat the days of veneration much like ordinary days, so we end up with lots of ordinary days and not so many days worthy of veneration.

The Wan Phra offers us a quiet time, a day for stepping back from the busyness of our ordinary activities. Here at Abhayagiri, we consistently encourage everyone to do that. For instance, we remind the community to refrain from turning on the computers or continuing with work projects. The Observance Day is a time to step back and keep the mind from being cluttered with these kinds of activities.

By truly observing the Wan Phra, we have a regular day set aside for reflection, a day to ask ourselves, *What do I take as a refuge? What is worthy of veneration? How well do I interact with the world around me? How might I cultivate virtue and integrity? How do I want to live my life?* Reflecting like this is not aimed at setting the highest possible standards for ourselves; it's not for trying to achieve theoretical ideals. It's simply to recognize what's useful—what works to decrease the discontent and suffering in our lives. Discernment of that nature, cultivated on Observance Days, motivates us to turn toward relinquishment, giving up, and letting go of things. This is central to the Buddha's teaching and to the very ethos of our practice.

Observance Days are an opportunity to step back from the busyness of ordinary activities, to reflect on our lives and practice, and to cultivate letting go. When used in these ways, they truly become days worthy of veneration.

Stepping Into the Rain

Ajahn Amaro • November 2009

When the weather turns wet and gray like this, the world is a bit less inviting outside, and it's easy to follow the natural instinct to seek shelter and find a cozy spot. We might find ourselves hanging around in the kitchen, the library, or the monks' office. It starts off with waiting for the rain to ease off, then an hour goes by, then two hours. We can end up spending hours doing a bit of unnecessary emails or thinking, *Well, maybe I'll make that phone call, maybe I'll take a look at this or that website.* The whole afternoon goes by with us chatting away with each other, waiting for the rain or the mood to change. This is a good way to waste time.

For the monastics here who have dwellings off in the forest, as well as for the people who are staying here as guests, it's good to recall the basic principle that we have of not gravitating toward the communal cozy spot or a place where there are good chatting opportunities. Once the meal is finished and the washing up is done, unless we have some urgent or significant business that requires our attention in the afternoon, we should pack up our things and go back to our dwellings.

It takes a certain resolution to walk out into a wet, gray afternoon, but once we are back in our dwellings, we find that solitude is the most delightful and helpful of companions. It takes an effort to turn and walk toward that. As the winter season is setting in with gray, misty, wet, cool weather, I strongly encourage people to refrain from huddling in that cozy spot looking for human company and cups of tea, and to instead step out into it. Go back to your dwellings. Spend time alone. Develop the path and turn your efforts toward the realization of Nibbāna. This is what we're here for.

The alternative to doing that is always available to us—the particular conversation we're interested in, this nice, cozy spot to settle in—the comfortable alternative. If we simply default to what's comfortable, what's interesting, the flow of a casual contact, hearing the news, looking for something to do, being engaged in something—anything—then we're really wasting our time. It's not helpful. It doesn't conduce to insight, concentration, or liberation—which is the purpose of this place and why this community exists.

We're not here to exchange information, contact others, or plan menus. Of course, these things have their place. They're all part of the everyday process of helping with the construction and maintenance of the buildings and with the cooking of food. But all these necessary tasks and all the extraneous little bits and pieces that demand our attention are not the purpose of our lives here. Those tasks and duties are merely the means by which we're fed and sheltered, supplying us with the requisites. Our lives here are for the purpose of developing the path and realizing Dhamma.

As the season changes and it becomes cool and damp, don't be blind to the influence the weather exerts over our minds. Take the opportunity to seek solitude, non-engagement, seclusion. These are the elements of the path that conduce to realization. These are some of the qualities that benefit and support our decision to live in this place, shave our heads, put on robes, keep the precepts, follow the routines and disciplines. And if we want to fulfill the true purpose for which we have come here—to realize the Dhamma—then we need to take the initiative, we need to back up our commitment with actions that match this greatest of all aspirations.

Reframing an Opportunity to Give

Luang Por Pasanno • October 2012

In one discourse, the Buddha speaks about the great gifts we give to countless beings by keeping the precepts. Through diligence in virtue, using the precepts to guide our conduct, we offer security to other beings—freedom from danger, fear, and animosity. These are great gifts, indeed.

Similarly, in terms of our daily lives in the monastery, it's helpful to reframe what we do and how we approach life so that we look at our activities as opportunities to give gifts of service. We can give a gift of service by doing a task that needs to be done instead of waiting for somebody else to do it. Rather than attending the morning *pūjās* and group practices because we feel they are being imposed from the outside, we can take our attendance as an opportunity to give a gift to the community by supporting and encouraging each other in practice. There can be a completely different relationship with how we deal with our schedules if we are willing to view them in this way. Rather than considering our duties and chores as onerous tasks we have to put up with, we can relate to them as an opportunity to give a gift that sustains the monastery and the supportive community we live in together.

We mustn't relate to the practice like wage laborers. If we think of ourselves as working stiffs trudging through the practice to get our paycheck at the end of the week, then there's not much joy or wisdom arising from what we are doing. But when we relate to the practice as a series of opportunities to give what's beneficial to others, then it is in all respects a different matter, it has a completely different feel. And of course, as with any gift, the first beneficiary is ourselves. When we relate to the training and the life we are leading in terms of giving, it uplifts our hearts.

Your Last Day Alive

Ajahn Yatiko • July 2012

During this morning's meditation I was reflecting on the sutta, Mindfulness of Death (AN 6.19) where one monk tells the Buddha he keeps death in mind once a day thinking that he might live that much longer to contemplate the Buddha's teachings. Another monk says he keeps death in mind several times a day, and yet another monk brings death to mind every minute or two. The Buddha says each one of these monks is dwelling heedlessly. One of the monks present says he contemplates that he might die in the time it takes for an in-breath or an out-breath. The Buddha commends him for that. After all, we could die on an in-breath, before breathing out. And with every out-breath, we could die before breathing in again. This is a powerful reflection. It brings the mind into the present moment in a striking way.

The Buddha described a group of five unskillful mind states that hinder the mind. These five hindrances are: sensual desire, ill will, sloth and drowsiness, restlessness and anxiety, and skeptical doubt. Taken to a deep level, this reflection on death can cause the hindrances to be in abeyance, because the hindrances almost always involve the passage of time. If the mind is in the present moment, and if we recognize that death could come this very instant—with the snap of a finger—then there's no time for the hindrances to arise.

For many of us, this is an old reflection. One way you can give it new life is to assume that this is your last day alive and that your moment of death will be tonight at the stroke of ten. How will you spend your day if this is your last day alive? You might say to yourself, *If this is my last day alive, I don't want to spend it on self-centered habits. I don't want this last day of my life to be marred by being heedless or by taking for granted this human form, this opportunity, this community, or by concerns about my personal health.* Behaving in those ways on the last day of your life would be tragic. You might also acknowledge the ordinary and practical aspects of life, saying to yourself, *I still have things I have to do today. I need to do chores and go to work. Let me do this in a way that's going to be an offering so that I can give of myself. I can support the monastery or help some people.* And finally, you might say, *Today is my last opportunity to free the heart from the defilements. Let me do my best.*

That's why we're here—to free the heart from greed, hatred, and delusion. Sometimes we can get lost in judging our meditation—*My samādhi is not good enough.* Although our meditation is very important, we forget that the whole reason we're meditating is to free ourselves from greed, hatred, and delusion. The depth of our samādhi practice or the experience of a profound insight is only significant because it supports that freedom. So we can reaffirm our intention to be free of greed, hatred, and delusion, to be content with our experience. For some of us, if not many of us, no matter how difficult our situation is—our health, our position, or our mental states—it's not so bad. It could be much worse. It's enough to be content with. This is simply where we find ourselves in this moment. This is where our kamma has put us. And it is possible for us to be content with our situation and to use it to free ourselves from the defilements.

When we contemplate death and think we have to overcome the defilements—which we do—remember that one of the defilements we have to overcome is discontent with ourselves. It's so common in this culture for people to find fault with themselves, to find it difficult to accept themselves. This manifests itself in so many ways. Sometimes we can see this trait in people who are conceited. Often that conceit is a mask for a lack of self-acceptance.

As this could be our last day alive, we can look at this dissatisfaction, discontent, or lack of self-acceptance and let it go. There's no time to waste. We don't have time to indulge in things like that. To a certain extent we need to be strict and firm with ourselves—*Things are okay. I'm okay. Everyone else here is okay. I am good enough and they are good enough, and I don't have to make a problem of who I am or who other people are.* We can let go of all our critical tendencies; they simply don't matter.

What does matter is that we look into our own hearts to see whether we find conceit there, a self-centered quality. Is there pride, ambition, anger, judgment, or self-righteousness there? That's why we are here—to look into our own hearts. We're not here to look at the structures and forms, like the monastery or other people's actions. None of this matters. The details don't matter. The monastery can be beautifully efficient and well structured, or it can be chaotic, strange, confusing, and disharmonious. All that, to a certain extent, doesn't matter. What is paramount is looking into our own hearts and asking ourselves, *Am I experiencing suffering or stress? What can I do to understand it? What can I do to encourage wholesome states of mind and decrease the unwholesome states?*

This is our work, and we don't have that much time to do this work, because we never know how much time we have or when we're going to die. So we need to take this reflection seriously, and to allow it into our hearts.

Desire Creeps In

Luang Por Pasanno • August 2012

It's worthwhile to watch the habits of desire and craving that keep creeping into the mind. Really notice and pay attention to desire, because it's insidious.

This isn't meant as a commentary on anyone's inability to recognize or understand desire or to work with it, but simply to say that it takes our concerted attention and a willingness to investigate to see how desire keeps creeping in. Most importantly, we need to be patient and willing to work with the different ways that desire comes up. Don't assume that because you've made a resolution, *Oh, I really want to free myself from desire,* that it's not going to manifest in various ways. Try to be very practical and attentive. Desire always seeks an object— that's the way the mind works. It goes to an object and becomes interested.

A prime example is the desire for food. In one psychology study I read, researchers tested two groups: one with fewer varieties of candy put out in front of them and one with more varieties of candy. Participants in the group with the increased varieties of candy ate sixty-nine percent more. One of the issues this may illustrate is how desire can increase our habit of craving based simply on seeing a greater variety.

I read about another researcher who'd written a paper on desire and advertising. One day he was in a supermarket checkout line ready to buy a sealed box containing ten packs of chewing gum. The box was labeled something like, "Ten Packs for Two Dollars." A colleague who was with him at the time said, "Hey, you've just written a paper on this!" People get pulled into such things. They see "Ten for Two Dollars" and think, *Wow, just twenty cents each—what a great deal!* They might not want to buy one pack for twenty cents, yet they get hooked into buying ten! It's merely marketing stimulating desire. So even a researcher who'd studied and written about this very thing—even he was hooked. Desire comes up.

That's just the way the mind works. Recognize that it's not personal, it's simply that desire seeks an object. Our job is to be attentive, reflective, and willing to investigate, to watch how desire keeps hopping around looking for an object, looking for something—anything—it can be attracted to.

We investigate, but not in a harsh way. We do this by taking an attitude of curiosity about desire, rather than feeling we have to run around with a sledgehammer and annihilate it. By paying attention to desire and recognizing what desire is doing, we can see how silly it is when we get hooked. You can ask yourself, *How dumb can I get?* That's the way to step back from it—by seeing desire clearly and not making a problem out of it.

The Whole of the Holy Life

Ajahn Karuṇadhammo • June 2013

With many people away, it's so quiet I can hear the water dripping over the sound of our breathing. We can have our own little retreat here today, which is always the way it is here regardless of the day. We can use every opportunity to practice mindfulness—to be aware of where our body is and what our mind is doing and ask ourselves, *Is this a skillful state of mind or is it an unskillful state of mind? Am I distracted? Am I in touch? Am I so absorbed in what I'm doing that I am not really seeing what's going on with the people around me?*

The title of Luang Por Pasanno's daylong retreat at Spirit Rock today is "The Whole of the Path: the Fruits of Spiritual Friendship." Many people know the sutta where Ānanda says to the Buddha, "The Saṅgha is half of the holy life," and the Buddha replies, "Don't say that Ānanda; it's the whole of the holy life." The opportunity to practice with people is one of the unique features of our community. Where would we be if we didn't have support from people when we are having difficulties or the feedback from people when we are missing the mark? The qualities of mindfulness, self-awareness, and sensitivity to other people are strengthened with the reflective guidance of spiritual friendship. Many of us are in need of individualized guidance for our training, and we support each other in this. We embody the sense of community and the sense of care and concern for each other. This is where the fruits of living in a community can truly be seen, especially in juxtaposition to people who lack support and have difficulties going it alone.

It can sometimes be challenging to rejoice in and take advantage of the opportunity to practice within a community. Because of this, it is useful to remind ourselves that it may not be here forever. Circumstances change, communities change, and we never know where we are going to find ourselves next. If we keep this in mind, we can use the opportunity we have here to be sensitive to each other, to be mindful around one another, to orient ourselves to our present experience, and to feel a sense of appreciation for the community we live in.

Leave No Trace

Luang Por Pasanno • June 2012

There's an idiom I appreciate from the Zen Tradition which is simply stated: "Leave no trace." It's an attitude ascribed to persons who do everything with clarity, efficiency, and mindfulness. It's helpful to cultivate this attitude, both as an ideal within the mind and also in terms of the little things we do—paying attention so we do not leave a trace behind us when we're engaged in our daily activities. This can be helpful even with very simple things like preparing for *pūjā* or getting ready for work. Wherever we go, we don't create a mess, we leave things neat and tidy. After washing our robes in the washing room, we wipe up the water around the sink; we make sure things are clean and tidy when we leave. Leaving our *kuṭi*, we ask ourselves if everything is neat and tidy. We see that everything is done in a circumspect, crisp, and clear manner. In this way, we can cultivate an attitude of leaving no trace.

There's an image for that in the Zen Tradition. Apparently, when turtles walk, their tails swing back and forth, sweeping away their footprints. That image suggests not leaving a trail of debris behind us when we walk from one place to another. Sometimes when the monks are getting ready for pūjā or having tea in the monks' room, they open and close the cupboards without thinking of others who can hear this. For those of us sitting in the Dhamma Hall next door, it's bang-crash-bang-crash-bang-thump-thump. So we need to be sensitive to the impact we have on those around us and try not to leave a trace of noise. In terms of our relations with people, we can reflect on the things we say by asking ourselves, *What kind of trace am I leaving in this conversation by the comments I've made?* With our internal processes we can ask, *What kind of trace am I leaving in my mind due to the moods I've picked up or the attitudes, views, or perspectives I'm holding?*

Instead of leaving behind the debris of our mental, spoken, and bodily actions, we can cultivate an attitude of leaving no trace. One image used for an enlightened being is a bird that leaves no tracks in the air. That's a great reminder for us as we go about our daily tasks and activities.

Why Am I Talking?

Ajahn Amaro • November 2008

I've been reflecting on the realm of right speech, an area in our lives that very swiftly gets carried away on the wind. Just as autumn leaves off the oak tree end up all over the landscape, so too our resolution to be more attentive and more mindful of speech gets carried away on the winds of circumstance. We might listen to a Dhamma talk on right speech and take in the various principles expressed by the teacher, but when we encounter each other we find ourselves wanting to comment on some event in the day that we've seen, heard, or read about. We overhear a conversation between others and find ourselves hanging around the edges, eager to chime in and say, "Oh yeah, I heard about that ... yada, yada, yada." And then off it goes. This is one of the perennial issues of community life.

The other day someone was quoting the little signs they have at Wat Mettā. One of them is the acronym WAIT: *Why Am I Talking?* We can apply that sort of inquiry even before we start talking: *Why do I need to talk? Is the world going to be a better place if I chime in at this point? Why do I want to get involved? Is it merely to engage for the sake of engaging? Is it an urge to burn some energy and connect? Is it just to fill up space? Is this actually going to be a benefit? Is this going to unite or divide? Is this going to bring clarity to others? Can I restrain the urge to comment, to speak, to put forth some opinion or some perspective?*

We're a very large community these days. The monks' room has many people passing through at different times—just before morning *pūjā*, at morning teatime, preparing for a morning meeting, during bowl setup, preparing for the work period, getting changed after the work period, cleaning up after the meal, enjoying evening teatime, before and after evening pūjā. It's good to be aware that the conversation we think we're having with just one person in the monks' room is actually involving other, unseen people, since the Dhamma Hall on the other side of the wall is like an echo chamber for the monks' room. This is especially apparent if things are quiet in the hall and there are loud conversations going on in the monks' room. Of course, sometimes there are things really worth talking about. But often, it's simply random chatter and only for the sake of engaging. So I encourage us to apply mindfulness and consideration, asking ourselves, *Is this really worthwhile? Am I considering that there are probably several people in the Dhamma Hall who will have to listen to all this? Is this something that's really worth sharing with so many people? Do I need to engage in this, or can I put it aside?*

In this way we can notice our accustomed patterns and see what situations draw us into pointless engagement and continuous verbal proliferation. When we learn to recognize those situations, we can take action to put ourselves somewhere else. Go sit on the porch, sit on the bench outside, or come into the Dhamma Hall. We can choose solitude over putting ourselves in close quarters where talking and pointless chitchat tend to launch themselves. This is one of the simplest and most direct ways the Buddha encouraged the development of mindfulness and the restraint of the *āsavas*, the outflows. We don't put ourselves in situations where that outflowing is going to be encouraged. We put ourselves somewhere else. It's very simple. We're not creating the conditions whereby a lack of restraint is being encouraged. Rather, we're inclining toward containment.

Every so often we need these kinds of encouragements to look at our own habits and involvements. When we make the effort to restrain and take the opportunity to disengage, then we can see for ourselves the results: how much quieter and settled the mind becomes. There's no need to remember the pointless chitchat or inquire about information that's not really benefiting our lives. We can recognize for ourselves, *Look how much more peaceful my mind is while I'm sitting, how much more easeful it is on the worksite when my mind isn't muddling around with all of this verbal engagement.* To start with, we can learn to WAIT.

The Lesser Discourse on
the Hole in the Ceiling

Ajahn Jotipālo • November 2012

In the earlier days, the Dhamma Hall was not quite as nice as it is now. One day Ajahn Amaro was giving a talk when it was raining really hard, just as it was this morning. As he was speaking, water started to leak from the ceiling and drip down right in front of where I'm sitting now—in pretty much the same place as the current leak we are having. Ajahn simply kept on giving the talk. It wasn't as if nothing was happening, but the new leak became part of the talk's theme of unexpectedness and uncertainty. I think we titled the talk "The Greater Discourse on the Hole in the Ceiling." The title alone made it memorable.

A little drip like that may look like a minor issue, but if there's a little drip inside, there's a hole someplace on the outside. Maybe there's a hole underneath a shingle and the water is getting in and flowing down into the rafters. The hole could be anywhere—it could be twenty feet away from where the water is dripping into the hall. That water is coming down and it's taking the path of least resistance. Maybe it hits a two-by-four and goes a different direction, then twenty feet later it hits another two-by-four. Meanwhile, inside the room here, the leak looks like it might be from a little hole in the ceiling that we could fix by putting a piece of tape over it. But a proper fix can be quite complicated, and if it's not taken care of quickly, then it's possible that all the water up there could saturate the drywall ceiling boards and the whole ceiling could collapse. So even what looks like a little drip can be quite serious.

This is often the case with a seemingly little issue like that. We can always put a towel on the floor and ignore the drip, or use a bucket temporarily as we've done right now. But the wise thing to do is investigate what's wrong and come up with an appropriate plan to fix it. That could mean finding its root cause and fixing it ourselves, or calling in a professional to help.

The same is true in living the holy life, in our meditation practice, and in developing Dhamma. There might be something on the surface, manifesting in our behavior or attitudes—something that we notice but others don't. Or maybe other people notice something about us, but we don't notice it ourselves. It could be minor. But if there is some troublesome issue that is the underlying cause, it can fester and grow. It can create many difficulties and problems for us and for other people. These things do need addressing. When something arises that requires our attention, we first acknowledge it as being an issue, and then investigate the extent of the problem it presents.

In some cases, we might not be able to fully see the problem or its cause, or we may suspect the problem is bigger than what we can fix ourselves. So with our Dhamma practice, when we have an inkling of that, it's important to enlist others for help—maybe a teacher who can look at the problem and help us work with it, undermine its cause, and eventually master it. That is how we can prevent a little leak in our practice from causing a large amount of suffering.

We can remember this talk as "The Lesser Discourse on the Hole in the Ceiling."

Slowing Down the Busy Mind

Luang Por Pasanno • June 2013

Even when we live in a monastery, the mind tends toward busyness and proliferation. This is a natural habit of the human mind. We can make ourselves conscious of that—not through a force of will, trying to squelch or annihilate it—but through understanding the mind's natural habits and the tendencies we carry with us. We can work with them in a skillful way. For instance, the mind tends toward speeding up and gaining momentum. When that happens, we can consciously slow down and pay attention. Sometimes this means physically slowing down, not to the point of irritating everybody around us, but also not getting pulled into a sense that, *This is important. There's not enough time. This has to be done now.* When we slow down, we can notice what happens, which is that we see things more clearly.

I've ridden in a car up and down Tomki Road to and from the monastery countless times. These last few months I've been walking on the road every day. It's a very different experience than riding in a car. When we ride in a car, we might think we see or know Tomki Road quite well, but because we're going so fast, we don't really see things clearly. By slowing down and walking, I've been experiencing many more of the nuances and details of the road, and there's more clarity as well. It's similar with the mind. We can learn how to slow it down, so that when we're engaged in activity, we can better attend to what we're doing. We slow down the impulse of getting swept up in the mind when it's worried, when it's proliferating, or simply chattering away. Of course, it's not necessary for the mind to chatter away like this, but as long as we're able to distract ourselves with that sort of thing, we feel it's okay. This is not a great program for a practitioner!

Instead, we encourage ourselves to slow down. In particular, when we're not engaged with work or duties, we can slow down by using walking and sitting meditation. We consciously slow down by bringing attention and awareness to the nuances of sight, smell, taste, touch, mental objects, and to the nuances of body, feeling, perception, mental formations, and consciousness. Those things—the six kinds of sense contact and the five aggregates—are what we use to create the sense of self and "me" and to solidify our moods and impressions into habitual tendencies. So we slow down enough to see them clearly. Learning how to slow down is quite simple, and it provides us with many direct and beneficial effects.

Small Choices Lead to Big Decisions

Ajahn Yatiko • November 2012

A lot of big decisions we make in life are dictated by the many small decisions we make on a daily basis. That can be a very powerful reflection, and one to keep in mind.

In the book *Crime and Punishment* by Dostoyevsky, the main character offhandedly fantasizes about killing a certain woman and stealing her money. He's not really serious about it but he asks himself, *What if I were serious?* He plays around with the idea, but realizes that he's certainly not committed to the idea, and decides not to proceed any further. But then, without even being aware of it, through a host of minor decisions, he manages to put into place various minor conditions that make the murder a real possibility. He goes from thinking that murdering the woman is ridiculous to feeling like he has no choice in the matter. He has to commit the act and so he does. It's like setting in motion an avalanche: a little movement here, a little there, doing this, doing that—then all of a sudden those seemingly minor conditions come together and produce a catastrophic result.

So it behooves us to reflect on the little choices we make, the small, moment-by-moment decisions triggered throughout the day by the various situations we find ourselves in. This reflection is intended to encourage us to be more circumspect about all those small choices. We need to remember the causative potential of a choice we make in a moment of heedlessness. It might seem like a small matter—and it might indeed *be* a small matter—but when coupled with other small matters, the cumulative effect can have a great impact. We can feel that external circumstances have trapped us into making a big decision in which we have no choice. But external circumstances aren't the culprits. We are. It was all those little, heedless choices we made along the way.

I'm a Lot Freer Than You Are

Luang Por Pasanno • June 2012

Yesterday, a group of us went over to the City of Ten Thousand Buddhas for a commemoration of Master Xuan Hua's fiftieth anniversary of coming to America. This morning while I was sitting, I remembered something said by Doug Powers, a long-time disciple of Master Hua. He had mentioned yesterday that Master Hua would both tease and challenge the students who came to study with him in the sixties and seventies, because at that time there was a strong ethos of people seeking freedom in many different ways. Master Hua would say, "You think you're free, but I'm a lot freer than you are." Our ways of trying to measure freedom—by trying to do what we want; as well as when, how, and where we want to do it—assumes that these ways will result in our experiencing freedom. In putting forth that challenge, Master Hua was questioning how people can measure freedom when they are still following their greed, hatred, and delusion. How can they be free when that's the case?

For all of our attempts to be free or peaceful or whatever, we still let greed, hatred, delusion, clinging, craving, and confusion not only follow us along, but push us from behind, conditioning how we react, respond, and interact with the world around us. If we spend our time scattered, impulsive, compulsive, and then sit in meditation a few times a day hoping to be peaceful or free, what we find is that the whole juggernaut of our daily actions dogs us around, and we get completely swamped with the flow of our habits and reactions in the mind.

By using the Buddha's path of practice, bringing mindfulness into our day-to-day activities, we encourage a certain clarity, precision, and circumspection with the things that we do. By doing this, we bring some measure of freedom from greed, hatred, and delusion into the little activities we engage in everyday. For example, when we clean up after the meal or after teatime, what is the first impulse? Sometimes it's simply to get up and move on to the next thing, engage in conversation, or whatever. We get swept up in our habits of mind. We need to create a container for our habits, so that we can see them more clearly and understand how we can circumvent or relinquish those tendencies. The tendencies of our trying to get what we want, following our views and opinions, reacting out of irritation or aversion—all of these tendencies are lacking solidity. But as long as we keep reinforcing them, believing in them, and following them, then these unwholesome habits grow and sustain themselves. We need to learn how to use the skills of mindfulness and wisdom to put a wedge into the wheel of our habitual unskillful tendencies, to slow them down, see them clearly, and recognize that we have options. We have a choice and we can either relinquish those habits or go against their grain.

Mindfulness and Concentration

Ajahn Karuṇadhammo • August 2012

Yesterday at teatime, we were talking about right concentration, *sammā samādhi*. One of the guests staying here had a question about *sati* versus *samādhi*—mindfulness versus concentration. It's a good subject to reflect on because we can sometimes be hard on ourselves when we are trying to concentrate our minds and the practice doesn't feel like it's going so well. This can happen when we have some fixed ideas about the nature of concentration. As Luang Por Pasanno says, even the word *concentration* taken by itself has a connotation of a narrow focus that's exclusive of other experience. He used an analogy between this tray here and samādhi. The tray is a good example of samādhi in that we need a firm foundation. The glass on the tray doesn't form a strong base like the tray does. In samādhi we are looking for a tray rather than a glass. After he explained this—a few minutes later—the glass spontaneously burst in front of us. I don't know if it was merely by chance, but it was a well-timed example of the instability of that glass samādhi.

It's good to keep in mind that sammā samādhi is dependent on and supported by the right application of the other path factors, specifically right mindfulness and right effort, but also all of the other factors: right view, right intention, right action, right speech, and right livelihood. All of those factors have to be in play for samādhi to be right concentration. It is not independent of those other factors and when we don't have significant amounts of time for intense, long periods of formal sitting meditation, the work we do with the other factors of the Eightfold Path forms that firm foundation, making it a broad base of practice. To begin with, we have to have right view, which starts with the knowledge that the actions we take in body, speech, and mind all have an effect in firming up that foundation and establishing peace within the mind. How we act throughout the day—the mindfulness we have when walking, doing dishes, working outside, working in the office and the attention we bring to what we're doing, even though it is quite active and engaged—helps to form that firm foundation.

When we skillfully practice the Dhamma, all of those factors work closely together and act as a base for that type of collectedness of mind. It's not a forced activity. We engage throughout the day with all the other aspects of the Noble Eightfold Path, so we have a greater ability to enter into a quiet, collected, enjoyable, peaceful state of mind. This concentration is not a result of having to go into sensory deprivation or exclusion of all experiences so we have a few moments of peace. That's not the kind of samādhi that is going to be stable, long-lasting, or even enjoyable. When we go through periods of practice that don't seem very fruitful or when we feel our minds will never settle down, we can bring to mind that the sitting practice and development of concentration is an important part of practice, but it's only one part of the practice. It needs to be supported by and firmly grounded in the other factors of the path as well.

Contented With Little

Luang Por Pasanno • November 2013

I recently read that in 1985—which is not so long ago—the average American purchased about thirty-two new articles of clothing per year. By 2010 it was up to almost sixty—and that was when the economy was in a tailspin. It seems many people are becoming more and more focused on consuming, without much consideration for what they already have.

By contrast, part of the ethos of living in a monastery as a *samaṇa*, a religious seeker, is developing the qualities of simplicity and frugality, and learning to be careful with how we use and reuse things. For instance, I have a cold now and have been blowing my nose quite often—I don't know how many times a day. So I try to emulate Master Hua, who would use the same tissue over and over again until it became apparent that it could no longer be used. I must admit that despite trying, I cannot match his austerity in this regard. However, it's a good illustration of frugality and taking care of what we use—we don't need to throw a tissue away after only using it once, but instead, we can keep reusing it until it's completely worn out. Simplicity and frugality are about doing little things like that: paying attention to all the things we use, taking care of them, and avoiding waste. Living like this helps protect the culture of modesty and contentment we've established here.

There's an idiom in Thai that refers to "one who is contented with little." Reflecting on this can inspire a life without complication. We can live very simply by being conscious of how we use things. Contrary to what one might think, this doesn't make us miserable. Contentment is quite the opposite of misery. Living in a conscious way like this can make us happier by fostering internal qualities that lead to ease and well-being. We realize that we don't require so many things to keep us happy and comfortable. It's an internal experience based on internal qualities.

The Best Potato Salad I've Ever Made

Ajahn Amaro • July 2005

We often think of insight meditation as something that we do as part of the formal practice. The usual instructions are to take some time to focus and concentrate the mind and when it's steady, to begin reflecting upon the flow of experience in terms of *anicca, dukkha,* and *anattā*—impermanence or uncertainty, unsatisfactoriness, and selflessness or things not being self. Luang Por Chah encouraged us to employ these themes of investigation and contemplation, not just on the meditation mat, but also throughout the day, during all of our activities. We can use these themes as constant companions to explore and process our own experience as we relate to the events of the day.

Ajahn Chah particularly emphasized the contemplation of anicca. He would often render the word *anicca* as uncertainty, rather than impermanence. When we think of things being impermanent it can have a remote or objective quality, whereas uncertainty describes the feeling of the mind and heart when we experience change and transiency. That's what we perceive—the feeling of uncertainty. We don't know. It's not certain because things are changing. It's not predictable.

This experience is easily accessible in our day-to-day lives, and is extremely useful to remember and sustain as a contemplation. We can understand this with something as simple as drinking a cup of tea prepared by someone else. As we bring the cup up to our mouths, we don't know how it's going to taste. There's that moment of almost palpable uncertainty. Or when we are on our way to perform some task, we might think, *I'm now heading up to the workshop to get this particular tool.* But if we reflect that finding the tool there is uncertain, then when we get to the workshop and find that in fact the tool isn't there, it's not a problem.

Although Ajahn Pasanno is leaving for Sacramento this morning, if we keep the uncertainty reflection in mind, then we can be clear that we don't really know if he is going to get there. The van driving him might have a burst tire or the drive shaft might snap somewhere along the highway, and then he would spend the day contemplating the heat element in the valley. Not that I wish for that to happen, but I can say to myself, *Oh, Ajahn Pasanno is going to Sacramento is he? Is that so? Really?* All we can know is that there's a plan for him to go to Sacramento. There's a plan to prepare the meal, and there's a plan to go into town. This much we know, but what will happen is uncertain. Are things really the way we judge them to be? It's not certain. This is not meant to create doubt and confusion, but the more we perceive each moment as uncertain, the more we see clearly that we don't know what will happen. We don't know what the outcome will be. We don't know if what we're doing will work or will happen the way we expect.

Similarly, we may judge the people around us and think that they are being greedy, aggressive, or selfish because of something we perceive they are doing. Later we might find out that they weren't being greedy, aggressive, or selfish—they were actually doing something that was helpful for somebody else. *It's merely my perception, my interpretation of a particular act, my presumption, my guesswork, or what I read into it.* When we see our assumptions clearly and find out that we were wrong about someone's motive, the framework of anicca can provide a quality of spaciousness and freedom for ourselves. The perception of anicca loosens the boundaries and obstructions we continually create through thinking, presumptions, opinions, judgments, expectations, and plans. We can learn to hold material objects, thoughts, feelings, and actions in the context of uncertainty. *This judgment is uncertain. This activity is uncertain.* When perceiving in this way, the heart is completely ready and open for the changes that can and often do occur.

If things go in a fortunate way, then we feel the pleasure of that. If they go in an unfortunate way, then we feel the painfulness of it. Ajahn Chah would say that clinging to happiness is just as bad as clinging to unhappiness. It's like trying to take hold of the tail of the snake rather than the head. If things go in a fortunate way, we might be clinging to happiness and say to ourselves, *Oh great, now I have it, this is excellent*—which means the heart has invested in that happiness. This happiness is like the tail of the snake. Even if we grasp the harmless tail, it's not very long before the head whips around and bites us. For example, if we've been preparing the meal, we might think, *Oh great, this is the best potato salad I've ever made. It's really good, I'm really pleased with this.* Then someone comes along, takes a mouthful and says, "Is it supposed to taste like this?" The anger or misery we feel is exactly proportional to the degree we had invested our happiness in the potato salad being just right, pleasing, and good. So we can learn to see that judgment as it's arising and consider, *Is the salad truly good? It's uncertain.* That way, we don't take hold of the snake's tail. If someone says it's bad, we can realize that it's simply their judgment, and the snake's head doesn't bite us. We might say to ourselves, *That person's a fool for thinking that.* But then we can see that this too is our own judgment. "Good salad" or "bad salad" is just the way we perceive things. It was uncertain to begin with. When we see this clearly, the causes for conflict, confusion, stress, and living a burdened life are no longer generated.

Having Faith in the Training

Ajahn Yatiko • September 2012

As monastics, it's worth keeping in mind where our focus is. It is not on worldly skills such as well-honed public speaking. The Buddha said that in former times, the monks who were respected and praised were those who lived and trained in the forest and put effort into practice, but later, respect and praise went to the monks who had good speaking skills. Skills, talents, and even an ability to give good Dhamma talks are praiseworthy, but what we are here for is the training. We are here to train the heart, and training the heart doesn't necessarily result in anything remarkable in terms of the external world. Training the heart results in sincerity, openness, peace, and mindfulness. We should keep in mind that this is why we're here. There's no other reason.

We need to have faith in the training—faith that the training works, faith that it will bear fruit. We might come across obstacles which could be with us for a long time, maybe for most of our lives. But the training will bear fruit—it doesn't make sense that it would not. We're putting sincere effort into cultivating mindfulness, restraint, and understanding, and we're dedicating ourselves to the principles of the holy life. The training has to bear fruit sooner or later, in this life or future lives. If those principles don't hold true, then as far as I'm concerned, life has no meaning. But because life does have meaning—because those principles do hold true—the best thing for us to do is give ourselves to the training, to the best of our capacities, and bear with the difficulties that arise.

When an obstacle to our practice arises, we need to remember not to throw the baby out with the bathwater. We do not have to disrobe or leave Buddhist practice forever. Something may have to change, and that might be a radical change in our views or in the way we approach practice. To deal with obstacles, we need to think creatively, outside the box, especially when we come up against a very persistent problem. Most importantly, the way through an obstacle is not to give up the struggle. Instead, we try to see it from a radically different perspective and carry on with the training. It's the training that gives meaning to life.

Choosing the Pāramīs

Luang Por Pasanno • July 2013

Several nights ago I gave a talk on the ten *pāramīs*, qualities that are helpful for cultivation and development: generosity, virtue, renunciation, wisdom, effort, truthfulness, resolution, loving-kindness, patience, and equanimity. Each is helpful to bring up as an alternative to a particular difficult or obstructive state present in the mind.

As a preliminary step, we can ask ourselves questions that pertain to these pāramīs in a general way. For example, *How do I want to orient myself and my practice? What principles of training do I feel need attending to?* When we think in terms of the pāramīs, the underlying connecting thread is making a commitment to or leaning toward what is wholesome and skillful, uplifting and brightening. We don't need to put a name on it or have a label for it. We can orient ourselves with these fundamental principles of wholesomeness and skillfulness and encourage ourselves toward these brightening qualities of mind. In a very elemental way, the function of these principles is to alleviate a tendency toward suffering.

When we're engaged in work or duties or have to deal with different personalities in our living situations, we have an opportunity to bring to mind these principles of training and to incline ourselves toward that which is wholesome and skillful. It's so easy to rationalize negativity, aversion, frustration, and a sense of *Oh, woe is me,* and really miss the point that we always have an option to choose. We can make an effort to keep exercising that option of choosing and inclining ourselves toward those principles of goodness. The pāramīs are ways of articulating those principles as specific qualities we can develop. We can also recognize the underlying impulse to opt for these principles of goodness, of wholesomeness, rather than resigning ourselves to attitudes of negativity and the things that thwart our spiritual aspirations. These are moment-to-moment choices, moment-to-moment opportunities for establishing a particular direction for our minds and our hearts. Ultimately, this direction will help us choose the pāramīs rather than something else.

Contemplation of the Body

Ajahn Karuṇadhammo • November 2013

The age-old themes of the body and contemplation of the body are again present for me. There is such a strong attachment to the body as self. I see this with my own experience and with so many of us here. There are those of us right now who are going in for physical exams, those with ongoing health problems, the issues with our friend Iris who is dealing with cancer, a number of people who need to see certain practitioners, doctors, and therapists for body issues, and six people going in for blood work tomorrow. We chanted the "Reflection on the Thirty-Two Parts of the Body" this morning. We do this reflection and examine the body because we are so strongly attached to it as either: who I am, something of which I am in possession of, or something over which I should have control. It forms a major part of who we think we are, and because of that strong attachment, when things go wrong we suffer greatly. That is why a large part of the practice is to try, over and over again, to alter the belief that the body is self or possessed by a self. If we can lessen that attachment over time, then little by little, when things go wrong, we do what we need to do to take care of the health of our bodies, but we don't do it with a sense of strong attachment, identification, clinging, pain, sorrow, lamentation, or grief.

We can practice this on an intellectual level and that's where it has to begin—bringing it in through the use of words and active reflection in a conceptual way. Yet how many of us let it reach a deep level, an emotional level, and possibly even further than that? Often, this level of deep understanding doesn't become apparent until something very serious happens. During those times we may come to understand that we have been dealing with body reflection in a shallow way. All of a sudden, the talks we have heard, the reflections we have done, all of the many times we have chanted the "Thirty-Two Parts of the Body" or some other body reflection, do not come into play. Where are they now?

The attachment to the body is so strong that we have to repeatedly bring it into consciousness at a very deep level. We do this by accepting that these bodies of ours are not things over which we have any control. We reflect on the process of aging, sickness, and death, let it sink in and at the same time, we look carefully at what is happening around us. For a person who is dying of a catastrophic illness, the death process is not just something that's out there, but something that is happening right inside that person's body. It could be the proliferation of cancer cells reaching different parts of the body, obstructing tissues and airways, and spreading to the bones and the brain. I can recognize that all of that is something that could very likely happen to me. Or some other disease will happen in this very body, to these internal organs, to all the parts we've been talking about, visualizing, and reciting. Each part will come to an end. They will all at some point cease to function, either one by one or at the same time. These parts of the body are subject to dissolution, decay, and decomposition and will return to the elements: earth, air, water, and fire, nothing more than that. Yet it all seems so real, so personal, and so "me," which is where the suffering comes in.

Bringing this reflection to heart is a significant part of daily meditation practice, both on the cushion and off. To do this we need to look around and bring this reflection into as deep a level of the consciousness as possible. This can seem like a monumental practice but it is possible. Over and over again we can gradually whittle away at the identification we have with the physical form and eventually gain insight into the impermanent and not-self nature of the body.

This Buddha Isn't the Same as the Old Buddha

Luang Por Pasanno • April 2013

Ajahn Chah used to emphasize the need for steadiness in our practice, especially with our application of effort—finding a level that pushes the edge a little bit, but is also sustainable and doesn't lead to our burning out. Sometimes we want to focus on tangible results, and it's certainly gratifying to feel we're really getting somewhere, that something's really happening. But I think it's much more important to focus on this kind of steadiness.

Steadiness requires patience. We need that patient quality of mind which is resilient and able to endure the different moods that come up—the highs of being exhilarated about the practice, and also the lows we inevitably experience. Moods oscillate like this; it's natural. So to achieve steadiness, patience must be applied along with effort.

The Buddha uses the image of water dripping very slowly into a huge earthen jug, drop by drop. If we focus on the individual drops, it may seem like nothing much is happening, as if the jug will never get full. But if the water continues to drip, slowly but steadily, the jug *will* fill up over time. It's unavoidable. In the same way, steadiness and continuity of effort paired together with patience will bring results in our practice, even if it seems like nothing much is happening.

There's no need to aim for a sudden, spectacular impact or achievement. It's tempting to hold onto the image of the Bodhisatta sitting under the Bodhi tree, resolving not to move until he had become enlightened, even if his blood dried up and his bones crumbled. We say to ourselves, *That's inspiring. I'll try to do that.* Once when a monk said that to Ajahn Chah, Ajahn pointed back at him and said, "Maybe *this* Buddha trying to do that isn't the same as the *old* Buddha." What Ajahn meant was that the Bodhisatta's resolve was the culmination of hundreds of thousands of lifetimes spent steadily and patiently building the *pāramī*.

So that's what we focus on—this steadiness of effort and patient endurance. Put them together and let them work for you.

The Gift of Space

Ajahn Yatiko • September 2012

It's a challenge to encourage people to grow in Dhamma. It's not a matter of simply telling people what to do or asking people to conform to a set of rules. We have to encourage and inspire people to dig deep within themselves to respond to situations in ways that are skillful. That often involves going against the grain. It's tempting to tell people what to do and to lay down a rule, but that's not the point.

If we see anger arise in other people, one way to quell the anger is to get really angry back and basically squash them with our words. That may shut them up, but there isn't much—if any—Dhamma present in that response. Another method is to manipulate them into stopping their anger by using subtle, temporary tactics, but that also doesn't help them grow in Dhamma. What helps is meeting their negative energy with space and loving acceptance. If we give them the space to reflect on their own anger, they might realize that anger is a form of suffering.

Sometimes we give space but sense that no investigation has come from it. If we give people space and they don't investigate their anger and irritation, there's nothing we can do about that. There's no guarantee that giving space to negative energy will resolve the situation, but it does give the other person the chance to work with it. And if we don't give space, if we respond to negativity with negativity, it's almost a guarantee that nothing profound will take place. Giving space is one of the best things we can do for people. It's noble. We don't condone what they're doing at the moment, but by giving them space, we encourage them to grow and gain insight into their own mental processes.

So this is a gift that we can give to others, a gift that others can give to us, and a gift we can give to ourselves as well. Whenever we receive this noble gift, we should use it as much as possible to lovingly look into the mind and see what actions cause suffering for ourselves and suffering for others.

Pesky Woodpeckers

Ajahn Amaro • August 2008

When we put up a building, we think it's our building, our Dhamma Hall, or our *kuṭi*, but no one informs the geckos, the lizards, and the other creatures in the forest. They think it's their place too. The woodpeckers were around long before humans showed up in this valley. This is the season when woodpeckers start to gather acorns and drill holes in the buildings, making little cupboards to stash acorns in. When people come along and put up a building, to a woodpecker, it's just a very odd-shaped oak tree. Before our beautiful new office building was even completed, the woodpeckers drilled a nice sequence of holes in this wonderful cedar trim all the way around the building. To a woodpecker, the trim is just a very nice, flat surface for stashing acorns with no bark or branches to work around. We think, *Pesky woodpeckers; they shouldn't be ruining our building.* But in reality, we've put up this attractive opportunity in their zone, and getting upset and irritated about it is simply proliferation—a story we've added on. As Luang Por Sumedho would often ask, "Who is being foolish?" Is it us or the woodpecker? In Thailand the rafters in the Dhamma Hall are great territory for wandering geckos. If a monk gets annoyed because he chooses to sit under the rafters and the geckos defecate on him, whose problem is that?

Our habit is to look at the world from a self-centered perspective: *My preferences. My priorities.* We look at our body in that same way: *My body has a right to be totally mobile, completely comfortable, pain free, and in an environment with the most desirable temperature at all times.* When that view gets intruded upon—when there's an infection, when the body is afflicted with a poison-oak rash, or when it is too hot or too cold—then we become reactive and that same self-righteousness arises: *This is an intrusion upon my space, my time, my convenience. I haven't got time for this; it shouldn't be like this.* If we believe those perceptions, then we endlessly create more *dukkha* for ourselves—this sense of dis-ease and dissatisfaction—because it's just the voice of self view, isn't it?

We don't tend to look at our body as a food source, but it is. It's a collection of organic matter. I never really understood this until I was living in Thailand. At first I was resentful of mosquitoes coming in and feeding on me, but at some point I realized that the body is a large, pungent magnet, like a big supermarket sign advertising a food source where the doors are always open. We don't think of ourselves like that. We think, *These darn mosquitoes are annoying me! These flies are landing on me!* But if we see that this body is simply a pile of heat-producing organic matter with interesting fumes, it makes sense that it would draw insects to it. If we shift the perspective a little, and drop that sense of self view, then we can similarly drop the burden of resentment, the feeling that life is being unfair.

That's the essence of the Middle Way—shifting from a self-centered view to the view that our bodies, the material world around us, and our minds are all natural systems—not "me," not "mine." And when we make that shift, when we adopt a view centered on Dhamma rather than on the illusion of an independent self, then the world changes quite dramatically.

So we can take care of buildings at the monastery, protect the body from insects, while at the same time not create stress or irritation or the sense of burden that comes with self view. If we understand that everything is part of the natural order, then "invasion" from the outside is impossible, because everything occupies the same territory; it's all of the same order. With this understanding, the heart relates to it all in a radically different way.

Paying Attention to Details

Luang Por Pasanno • May 2012

When bringing Dhamma practice into our daily lives, it's important that we pay attention to the ordinary little details around us. If we hold to a broad, nebulous "just be mindful" attitude, we're unlikely to be clear about what we're doing. So it's important to keep ourselves from overlooking things, especially while living in community as we do here at the monastery.

Through our attention to ordinary details, we cultivate an attitude of mindfulness that's sharp and connected with what's happening around us—an attitude that is central to our training. Over time, this attitude permeates the way we relate to our minds and our experiences. That's critical because our defilements don't advertise themselves by holding up big signs that say, "Greed! Hatred! Delusion!" We need to look closely if we're to discern and understand the nuances of the attachment and delusion we experience. If we haven't cultivated the habit of paying attention to details—both external and internal—if we don't put forth the extra effort required for that, then we'll miss many significant aspects of our practice.

The Buddha pointed to *yoniso manasikāra* as a vital part of the path. It refers to skillful and wise reflection and close attention to the root of things. This quality doesn't pop up by itself like a mushroom in the fall; it has to be cultivated. In our ordinary day-to-day activities, we can support this cultivation by again paying attention to details. We do this, for instance, by making a continuous effort to notice when any little thing needs doing, such as returning a tool to its proper place, and then doing what's called for, even if it's not "our job." When everyone pays attention and takes responsibility like that, the monastery functions beautifully.

The Buddha based this entire path of liberation upon the experience of dissatisfaction, discomfort, stress, suffering—*dukkha*. Paying attention to details is a doorway though which we can learn what leads to dukkha and what doesn't. While it may seem like a small thing, this attention is essential if we're to live our lives skillfully and in a way that opens us to the possibility of true peace and freedom.

Beautiful Work, Beautiful Mind

Ajahn Vīradhammo • October 2012

Whether it's sewing robes or making a footpath, the Forest Tradition has a high standard of workmanship. But quite often we're asked to do things we're not competent in or used to doing. There's a learning curve we all go through in the Saṅgha. If we've never had to do welding and we end up assigned a welding job, or if we've never been an abbot and we end up being an abbot, it becomes a real training in how we learn new skills.

One of the monks at Chithurst Monastery was a very good carpenter and cabinetmaker and in general, an excellent worker. He once suggested that one of the best ways to learn a manual craft or skill is to undo any mistakes we've made, rather than covering them up. I saw him do that several times. He would be building something quite complicated like a staircase and if he saw a mistake, he would reverse his steps until he'd gone back to the place where the mistake was made, and then he'd correct it. My tendency had been to keep going after making a mistake, and hope that no one would notice it. Watching this monk work I also noticed that once he had retraced his steps backward to correct some mistake he'd made, he tended not to make that same mistake in the future. Not surprisingly, his work was very beautiful.

Once I watched Luang Por Liem make a beautiful broom. It was a fabulous example of very mindful craftsmanship, his hands were so attentive and efficient. Luang Por obviously has the gift for it, but that gift has been greatly enhanced by his many years of training in mindfulness.

When our task involves working with others, it's a perfect opportunity to develop the beautiful skill of patience. For example, we may have a skill or aptitude for the task and already know how to do it quickly, but we're working with someone who is a bit clumsy and slow because he or she doesn't have that same training or aptitude. In that situation, we need to practice patience with each other.

Whether or not we already have the skills required to tackle a certain project we've been assigned, it's always rewarding to do things carefully and beautifully, as best we can. Abhayagiri's lodgings and buildings are quite beautiful. Whether it's the robe rail or the sleeping platform, they are all nicely done. I can appreciate everything it must have taken to complete these lovely works—the mindfulness and workmanship, the patience, and the willingness to learn.

Opening or Collapsing to Experience

Luang Por Pasanno • June 2013

As we apply our practice to the circumstances in which we find ourselves—whether we are working in the kitchen, out on the trails, or in the office—we apply mindfulness to the present moment while also connecting and establishing our continuity of mindfulness to the posture of the body. There's a natural tendency, as we engage in our work, to move forward and hunch. We can make this habit conscious, re-grounding and reconnecting with the body by opening up the chest and breathing comfortably. We are not trying to strut around with a military posture—we can open the body, the chest, and the heart base by expanding our posture. Another way to see it is opening up our presence to how we engage with the world around us.

With the habit to collapse in and slump forward we can try to continually bring in that sense of an expanding and spacious presence. We can pose little questions to ourselves as reminders: *Am I present? Am I here?* If we do this, we end up acquiring a continuity of awareness that is then brought into our sitting meditation. When we are sitting in meditation, if we are slumping and collapsing our posture and not really putting effort into the present moment, we tend to collapse in the mind as well. Ajahn Chah put a lot of emphasis on continuity and steadiness in practice and training. This is shown in the little things that we do and not in some sort of major heroic activity. We continue to place our attention on the body and the present moment with a sense of opening. It's an important attitude to carry into our daily practice.

Respecting Others' Boundaries

Ajahn Yatiko • May 2012

I had a significant learning experience about two or three years after I had ordained. A good friend of mine whom I ordained with was the monastery's stores monk. One time he went away for a week to Pu Jom Gorm, a branch monastery. During that time, I became the stores monk in his absence. I was keen to be helpful and do something supportive or generous as a show of kindness to him. So I cleaned up and reorganized the stores room, and I thought I did quite a nice job. When this monk returned a week later, he was visibly upset and took it as a personal comment or statement that he wasn't doing a good job on his task as the stores monk. This wasn't my intention at all. I saw some things that would be good to do, so I went ahead and did them, though I was not appreciated for what I had done.

In monastic life, it's important to recognize and respect other people's boundaries. In this case, if I had been more sensitive, I would have considered whether my cleaning and reorganizing the stores room would have affected my friends feelings by impinging on his role and duties as the stores monk. If I felt something should be done differently, it might have been better to have kept that to myself. It can be difficult for the stores monk if all of us expresses our opinions about the way he should manage his job. Or I might have waited until he returned, approached him, and asked if there was anything I could do to help. Then if he'd said something like, "Yes, what did you have in mind?" it might have been a good time to express an opinion while still respecting his boundaries.

To take another example, we hear the guest monk in the office giving some advice to someone over the phone, and we feel *we* know what should be said, and so we tell him what we think. This can be very burdensome for the guest monk. We have to think about boundaries, because there are many different tasks in the monastery: abbot, work monk, monastery secretary, guest monk, stores monk, computer monk, kitchen manager, chores monk, librarian, accounts manager, and so on. These tasks can take a fair amount of effort and patience to deal with. So it may be helpful for us—before we decide to "assist" someone or express our opinion about how a task should be done—to ask ourselves whether we are creating more of a burden for the person who has taken on the responsibility of doing that particular task.

The subject of boundaries goes beyond respecting each other's duties. There are also boundaries around physical space. How do we enter a room? When we walk into a room with people inside, how do we enter their field of awareness? Do we simply walk right in and announce our presence, or do we respect and appreciate the space in the room, entering with care?

There are also property boundaries. Let's say I was missing something I owned. I'm a senior monk and have an attendant. If I thought what I was looking for might be in my attendant's personal cupboard, I might ask him to look in his cupboard when I next see him. But I would never go through his stuff looking for something simply because I thought it might be there. It's a different story if it's an emergency, but in other contexts it's not something that I feel is the right thing to do.

Living in community as we do, we can think about boundaries and remember that we want to focus on our own practice rather than what other people are doing. As the Buddha explained, we shouldn't go outside our own domain into the domain of others, because if we do, Māra will get a hold of us (SN 47.6). We can think of this as understanding and respecting people's boundaries. So we do what we can to respect and honor physical boundaries like property, as well as the boundaries delineated by roles. In this way, we support harmony and well-being within the community.

Where Did It All Go?

Ajahn Karuṇadhammo • August 2012

Today is Beth's birthday. We were talking a few minutes ago about how quickly it all happens, how fast the time passes, particularly as one gets older. Time tends to telescope and move much faster with age. Beth mentioned her mother was recently looking in a shop and saw a reflection in the window. Her first thought was, *Who is that old lady?* Then she realized that it was herself! I remember a time when I was about ten years old and thought to myself, *Wow, in the year 2000 I'll be forty-five years old.* All of these experiences of time are very malleable and fleeting.

We can use this perception of time as a reminder that the life that we have is a certain length and we don't know how long it's going to be. It may not last beyond the next few minutes or it may go on for many, many years from now. The point is that we don't know. For most of the time in our lives we are either thinking about the past or projecting into the future. We miss the point that it's all happening right here in this moment.

We need to use a sense of urgency, knowing there is an aging process, illness, and death. We don't know when illness and death will occur. We only know that it will occur at some point in time. With this type of reflection we can develop a sense of urgency to encourage our minds to dwell in the present, because the present is where we have the ability to change and create favorable conditions for the development of our minds. It's not thinking about the past, having regrets about the past, or making projections into the future; it's about responding to what comes our way right here and right now in this very moment. Of course, it's easy to believe our thoughts, *Well, the time isn't quite right. Maybe when the conditions are better I'll start practicing seriously. I have plenty of time left and there are just too many responsibilities right now and too many goals I have to accomplish. As soon as I get this part of my life together then I'll really be able to practice.* But that's a kind of false thinking that we get ourselves into. It's a misperception that we're going to have all that time when the conditions are perfect, because the conditions are never going to be perfect. We have to take the opportunity right here and right now to take what's coming our way and work very closely with greed, hatred, and delusion.

It's not as if we're trying to create a different person in the future who will then be more skilled and capable, *If only I didn't have so much anger or craving . . . I'll work on that so in the future I will become somebody who can be much more free.* While it is true that things develop over time, it is the effort we put forth right here and right now, seeing our reactions and habits just as they arise that allows us to change our perceptions and understand our human experience. If we keep on putting it off, spending time regretting all the things we did in the past, or projecting into the future without paying attention to right here and now, then we've missed the opportunity to make a genuine change in our present experience. Realization and genuine shifts of perspective don't occur somewhere off in the distant future. They occur right now in this moment.

Nourishing the Spiritual Faculties

Luang Por Pasanno • May 2013

We just had Ajahn Dtun staying at the monastery, and he very generously shared teachings with us. For most people here, I think, his presence and way of being were uplifting and generated the arising of faith. Now, whenever faith or confidence arises in us—whether from the presence of a teacher or whatever the source—it's important to use that faith to benefit our practice. The wholesome result of faith is the inclination to apply effort or energy. In this way faith is nourishment for effort and energy in our practice.

These two qualities are among the five spiritual faculties: *saddhā, viriya, sati, samādhi,* and *paññā*—faith, energy, mindfulness, concentration, and wisdom. None of these factors stand alone. They support, feed, and nourish each other. We need to attend to saddhā—faith or confidence—in a skillful way, so that it helps nourish the qualities of effort, mindfulness, wisdom, and samādhi. Together these qualities bring a steadiness of mind, a clarity of awareness. In the suttas, the Buddha teaches that the spiritual faculties are a direct source of awakening. When we generate and nurture them, we are directly nourishing the conditions for awakening.

In his teachings, Tan Ajahn Dtun emphasized samādhi—concentration or collectedness of mind—the fourth spiritual power. In doing so, he also specified that the function of samādhi is to stabilize and steady mindfulness. Ajahn Chah taught this as well. This is important because it's easy for us to get caught up in our preconceptions about the various states of samādhi and their purposes. Having read or heard about samādhi states from various teachers, we may misunderstand the most important reason for practicing samādhi. Again, it's for the stabilization of mindfulness. When mindfulness isn't steady, we have to return to a wholesome meditation object and use formal exercises for developing samādhi, such as the mindfulness exercises described in the Satipaṭṭhāna Sutta.

Further, samādhi and mindfulness are mutually dependent—each nourishes the other. Samādhi develops through the continuity of mindfulness practice, and the stabilization of mindfulness requires a continuity of samādhi. The continuity of samādhi and the stability of mindfulness are essential components of the path to awakening.

Each of these wholesome and skillful spiritual faculties positively influences and supports so many aspects of the Buddha's path. We can get a glimpse of their power when we see them exemplified in the elder teachers whom we come in contact with. It's important that we take full advantage of these teachings and teachers. They are invaluable supports for our practice and spiritual cultivation.

The Real World

Ajahn Amaro • October 2009

What does a Buddhist monk know about the real world, anyway? It's a common question because there's a sense of the monastery being an isolated sanctuary where we say, "Goodbye cruel world," and then come into our beautiful, sacred space, and suddenly we're spiritual. That's a bit of a sweeping generalization, but it's often the way people think. What is a monastery? What is the purpose of a sanctuary like Abhayagiri? And what is the "real world?" Anyone who has stayed here for more than a few hours realizes that far from getting away from the real world, monastery life is designed to be a place where we meet that world—the real world of our own perceptions, preferences, fears, desires, and opinions.

Even those of us here might think, *Oh, there are so many difficulties in the world—social stresses, problems of climate change, the collapsing economy, so many suffering beings in the world. What am I doing in a monastery? How am I helping? Am I just trying to hide away from the real world?* Those are reasonable questions. But what we find at the monastery is that because there is a meeting with the real world of our own minds and bodies and the physical reality of our existence, we are, in an important way, more genuinely engaged with the real world than when we're running around outside. The blur of activity in an ordinary, everyday life, even when it is involved with compassionate and beneficial activity, can also entail being disconnected both from oneself and those around oneself.

Living in the monastery and undertaking monastic training is about bringing our attention to ordinary everyday activities. The way we carefully put two pieces of PVC pipe together, chop an onion, clear a trail, or edit a Dhamma talk, and the way we carefully bring our attention to each of those activities—attuning the mind to the present moment—is what creates a sacred space. That is what makes this place a monastery, rather than an aggregation of individuals following their own wishes, opinions, and habits. Sanctuaries such as this are a tremendous benefit and blessing to the world, because they let people know there are places where others will not lie to them, try to cheat them, try to flirt with them, get money from them, or wish them harm. This is a tremendous gift.

We may ask ourselves, *How am I helping the world by chopping onions or pruning branches on the trail?* When a reasonable doubt like that arises, it's important to realize that the intention to bring mindfulness, care, and the cultivation of unselfish conduct into these simple and apparently insignificant acts is a way in which we are helping the world. The very fact that this monastery exists at all, with a couple dozen people choosing to live and train themselves in this way—it does have an effect. It is a beneficial and guiding presence in people's lives all over the planet and is truly something in which to rejoice.

Developing Respect and Humility

Luang Por Pasanno • August 2013

Before the monastery was established, I can remember Ajahn Amaro telling me that there was a Thai monk in Fremont, Ajahn Maha Prasert, who was keen to see a forest monastery succeed in the Bay Area. Since the founding of the monastery, Ajahn Maha Prasert's support has been unfailing.

Generally in Thailand at the beginning of the Rains Retreat or a bit earlier than that, most of the monks in monasteries go together to pay respects to senior monks in the same province. This is important for a monastery and for one's individual practice. These trips are opportunities for showing respect and giving respect outside of one's own little circles as well as within one's circle. In America, we don't have many options, but we do have Ajahn Maha Prasert. We're fortunate, because he's a worthy monk to pay respects to.

When we reflect back on the discourse that the Buddha gave on the highest blessings, one blessing he points to is *gāravo ca nivāto ca*, the qualities of respectfulness and humility. These are qualities that bring forth the highest blessings. They engender the sense of not having to carry the burden of a sense of self all the time—which is an incredible burden. Sometimes we can lack humility and respect to the degree that we outwardly appear full of ourselves and carry our sense of self around, showing it off to other people—which is not very inspiring.

We have the opportunity to establish a sense of respectfulness and humility not just once a year, but in our day-to-day lives—how we live with each other, how we treat each other, and how we engage with the world around us. We can frequently think about meditation techniques and methodologies. But when we reflect on the qualities that help the mind become peaceful, we can see how often we overlook these fundamentals that are at the roots of our being—these qualities of respectfulness and humility that allow the mind to become quiet and at ease. If we've engendered these qualities within, then when we sit down to meditate, we don't have to wonder what techniques or methods will make us peaceful, because the peace is already there waiting for us.

Making the Embers Bright Red

Ajahn Yatiko • June 2013

Due to our past kamma, we have found ourselves in a Buddhist community with harmony and good feelings, and most importantly, we have teachings that are encouraging us in the practice and leading us to truth and peace. We have the space and time to practice and relatively good health, and our requisites are well provided. We can recognize this and appreciate the opportunity we have. This is a helpful reflection, but it is also important to have a clear insight into the extreme rarity of this kind of situation.

When we develop this insight, it's like waving a fan in front of a fire to make the embers bright red. We need to go over this insight and work at it until we really see it. We can do this by setting a goal, not so much to attain *samādhi* or to have perfect mindfulness, but rather, to arouse a clear, vivid sense of the urgency of our situation. If we are successful, and this insight arises, it can be very exhilarating.

When the embers are bright red from this insight, then it's like starting an engine; the engine takes care of itself once it gets going. We start this engine by making an effort to see the specialness of our situation, our environment, the teachings, and the comparative rareness of this experience. We can ask ourselves, *How many beings are in a situation where they are so tight up against the conditions of life that they can't separate themselves from those conditions and it just seems impossible to get a perspective on the Dhamma?* That's the case for the vast majority of beings in the universe. Go over this insight into the rareness of our opportunity, and work at it over and over again until the embers are bright red and the engine is humming along without effort. We can let the practice take care of itself from there.

This Pūjā May Be My Last

Ajahn Jotipālo • September 2013

There is a fairly well-known sutta where the Buddha indicates that one who contemplates death about every few seconds develops mindfulness of death heedfully, with diligence, while one who contemplates death every few minutes or more develops mindfulness of death heedlessly, with sluggishness (AN 8.73). It only takes two or three seconds for someone to die from an aneurysm. It's much the same with a massive heart attack or any number of other medical conditions and accidental calamities. We can be fully functional one moment, and dead two or three seconds later. So we have good reason to contemplate death quite often, as the Buddha suggested.

Sitting on the ordination platform this morning for *pūjā*, I had an unusually strong sense of how beautiful it was, just sitting there. I asked myself why I might be feeling this way. We are getting ready to go on a trip to Yosemite and there is a national disaster occurring just twenty miles from where we will be camping. When I looked online yesterday to check out the conditions, there were three major weather alerts for Yosemite Valley. One was a warning about severe thunderstorms, another was a flash flood warning, and the third warned about unhealthy levels of smoke in the air due to the large fires burning in the area. And of course, there was the risk of fire itself. I thought to myself sarcastically, *Oh, this looks like a wonderful place to go camping! Luang Por Pasanno is urging me to go and says it's a great opportunity. Does he just want to send me off to my death?* Sitting there during pūjā, I had the sense that it really could be my last pūjā on that platform.

This is true for every single one of us. Maybe you're not heading off to Yosemite, but death could occur at any time—when you're driving into Ukiah, taking the small diesel vehicle up the monastery road, or working in the kitchen where the gas oven might explode. We don't need to be obsessive or neurotic about death, but it is good to have it constantly in the back of our minds.

Just before coming to Abhayagiri, I used to be on the maintenance staff at IMS (Insight Meditation Society) in Barre, Massachusetts. I remember being strongly attached to certain opinions about the way things should be done with work projects there, such as using particular types of paint and cleaning products. These sorts of opinions were a major part of my consciousness in whatever project I was involved. But after leaving IMS and coming here, I realized that I didn't have a care in the world about what kind of paint they were using in Barre. My consciousness of being at IMS had, in essence, died—not in a negative way, but because I no longer had any input there.

When Ajahn Yatiko was the work monk here at Abhayagiri, he had to put a lot of effort into making sure that everything was done correctly on the work scene. But I have a suspicion that Ajahn Yatiko, now living in Sri Lanka, isn't worried at all about how we are handling the work scene at the moment.

These are some of the reasons why I think it's good to contemplate death. These contemplations are especially helpful when we find ourselves hooked into some minor thing we feel is so important. If we were diagnosed with terminal cancer, then some trivial issue or a difficulty with a particular person would probably seem insignificant. So I encourage everyone to frequently bring up these contemplations on death. And the next time you're sitting on the ordination platform for pūjā, enjoy the beauty there, and consider, *This pūjā may be my last.*

Approaching Gorillas

Luang Por Pasanno • August 2012

We are trying to bring mindfulness to our day-to-day activities. We need to keep reminding ourselves of that. It's easy to say to ourselves, *Just be mindful.* But we hear it so often that it can seem trite and can lose its impact. The practice of mindfulness, the application of mindfulness, learning how to direct mindfulness, are key foundations of our practice and training. Once we learn how to establish and balance mindfulness, we can more clearly understand the mind and its reactions.

The biologist George Schaller was the first person to study silverback mountain gorillas. People who read his studies were amazed that he was able to get close enough to the gorillas to observe their habits and social structure and even the primitive language they used. People would ask how he was able to achieve this. His answer was that he approached the gorillas in a manner that was very different from the way others had tried and failed: he never carried a gun. This allowed him to establish a trusting relationship with the gorillas and approach them with a sense of ease.

Now think of what our minds are doing all the time. We carry weapons around—our "guns" of views and opinions, our moods and biases, our tendencies toward reactivity, and all our extra baggage. They keep us from getting close enough to clearly see what the mind is doing, its underlying tendencies, or what its potential capability might be. We're not able to approach our experience mindfully.

We need to put down the weapons of our likes and dislikes, our views and opinions, and the constant chatter and commentary that we're always overlaying onto the world around us. These weapons constantly separate us from the world and from our experience. Once we've put our weapons down, we can take up the fundamental quality of mindfulness. We can pay attention and be aware without moving in with reactivity. That way, we can begin to establish a quality of real peace, while also learning to coexist with our own minds.

Can't We Always Be on Retreat?

Ajahn Karuṇadhammo • April 2013

We're still in the process of coming off our three-month retreat and adjusting to the different pace, level of energy, and engagement. I've been reflecting on some of the words I've heard from others and what I sometimes hear in my own head: *Why can't we always be on retreat? Why can't we always live this particular way? Can't we slow down and have more space and time for formal practice in the day?* The logical answer is that there's a monastery that needs maintaining. All the buildings we live in and the different things we need as requisites have to be looked after. That's the logical reason. If we didn't have Abhayagiri, we wouldn't have any place for retreat. So we all need to pitch in and help.

We're working on a greater perspective, a long-term goal in this practice, and our abilities to realize peace of mind need to be ones that aren't dependent on specific circumstances. We need to be able to develop mindfulness, clarity, and ease of living in whatever situation we find ourselves, whether it's retreat, engagement, work, or community. We're developing an all-encompassing freedom that can be realized in any circumstance, whether in quietude or engagement. One of the qualities that's so important in developing this is patience—not to expect big realizations or quick understanding. This is a gradual path and requires a tremendous amount of patience. It's not the kind of patience where we grit our teeth and simply bear with it, but rather, it is a spacious, wide-open acceptance of the way things are.

I remember as a very junior monk, a time when I had some difficult interactions with another community member. I was trying to strategize how to better cope with it and more skillfully handle the situation because there was a lot of frustration and anger arising in me. I tried the usual antidote, developing loving-kindness, but it wasn't working because there was a sense of resistance, strain, and aversion with trying to get rid of the particular circumstance. I realized that more important than directly responding with loving-kindness was cultivating a sense of patience—both for this other person and for myself—while I tried to develop the skills needed to handle and cope with the situation. Practicing with patience helped me see more clearly what my expectations were. It allowed me to be more open and I sensed, *Okay, this is deeply ingrained in me and it's going to take some time. It's not always going to be pleasant, but I need to open myself up to the circumstances and be a bit more spacious with it.*

That's what the quality of patience is all about. It's not a quality of gritting one's teeth and bearing with the circumstance until things get better, or bearing through the next nine months until we get three more months of retreat. It's about opening to one's experience and developing a sense of clarity and understanding that this is a long-term process. The more we can be patient with ourselves and with the practice in our living situations, the more we can open to whatever it is that comes our way and use it as a tool for learning about ourselves.

Nothing Bad Has
Ever Happened to Me

Luang Por Pasanno • November 2012

Gratitude is an important quality to bring to mind, because it's easy for the mind to focus on faults, flaws, difficulties, and obstructions. Whether it's external or internal—the things around us, or our own particular difficulties—it's easy to obsess on the negative. When we cultivate and bring to mind a sense of gratitude, it helps the mind direct attention to what is wholesome, skillful, and positive. It's not a small thing, because the mind requires a reserve and foundation of well-being, and gratitude is a very direct way of being able to establish that. We don't need to have everything go our way or get what we want in order to be grateful; the fact that we're alive, breathing, and conscious is a lot to be grateful for already.

Last night, one of the people at Yoga Mendocino mentioned the Jewish concept of a *tzadik*, a person who is an adept or a well-developed person. One characteristic of tzadiks is that they have a sense of gratitude. In the Jewish tradition, this would be gratitude to God. This reminded me of an eastern European Jewish story where a rabbi went to visit another highly respected elder rabbi in the Ukrainian Hasidic tradition. The visiting rabbi says to the elder rabbi, "In the Talmud it says we should be grateful and praise the Lord even for what is evil, let alone for what is good. How are we supposed to understand that?" The elder rabbi replies, "Go to my student, Zusha, over in the House of Study and ask him." So the visiting rabbi walks over to the House of Study and finds Zusha there, emaciated, filthy, and clothed in rags. He asks, "Zusha, how are we supposed to understand the saying from the Talmud that we should be grateful and praise the Lord even for what is evil, let alone for what is good?" And Zusha answers, "I can't tell you. I don't really know. Nothing bad has ever happened to me."

When we are established in the quality of gratitude, it buoys us up through everything. There are many logical reasons why we could feel that something is awful or not up to our standard. But from a different perspective, we have the life faculty and the opportunity to come in contact with wholesome experiences. We can make a choice with what is good and what is bad, what is conducive to happiness and well-being, and what is conducive to making the choices that lead to those wholesome qualities. That's something to be incredibly grateful for. We can generate that gratitude by paying attention to the inclination of our minds, by recognizing what our minds are doing and when we have lost this sense of appreciation. In seemingly difficult and trying circumstances, we can encourage those qualities of gratitude that allow us to understand that, for the most part, as Zusha suggests, *Nothing bad has ever happened to me.*

Taints to Be Abandoned by Using

Ajahn Yatiko • July 2012

In the Sabbāsava Sutta, All the Taints, the Buddha says we can abandon taints by using the four requisites—robes, food, shelter, and medicine in the appropriate way. It's an interesting reflection that taints are to be abandoned by consciously using the requisites. Even though we're renunciants and sometimes we have ideals about getting by with less robe cloth, sleeping outside, eating less, or some other idealistic standard, we always have to remember that the foundation of our lives is based on a very down to earth, grounded, and simple practice around robes, food, shelter, and medicine. Attending to these requisites with mindfulness and care helps us in our spiritual lives—that's the purpose.

A teacher once told me that when he eats, he does it as an act of loving-kindness to his body. He feeds the body because he's caring for it and expressing his desire to care for it. The body is quite fragile, and it can be helpful to reflect on whether we are relating to the body with loving-kindness or with a demanding attitude. Based on some ascetic ideal, we might live in a way that is not kind to the body, causing harm to ourselves. For the sake of our practice, we need to care for the body in a mature and balanced way, with kindness and discernment

Food is a valuable tool that allows for comfortable, easy living. We might identify with being really austere monks and regularly fast for lengthy periods of time. Or we might move toward the opposite extreme and take great delight in delicious food. In either case, we need to ask ourselves, *Am I caring for the foundation of my practice? Am I using the requisites wisely?*

Whether we are relating to the requisites from a sensual perspective or an extremely austere perspective, this is not the path the Buddha suggests. Rather, we can reflect on whether we are using the requisites in a way that supports our long-term practice, and adjust our behavior accordingly. That is a valuable reflection to cultivate, apply, and strengthen over the years.

A Sense of Self

Luang Por Pasanno • July 2011

Student: I'm trying to overcome a sense of self, but my spiritual quest seems to revolve around me trying to attain something. The thought of dropping my self seems like a snake swallowing its tail.

Luang Por Pasanno: That's the way it is in the beginning. It's a process of feeling it out. You have to play with it and work it out over time as you get better and better at it. It's important in the beginning to be in the right container and have good spiritual friends. These serve as supports. In the beginning you flail around a lot, but it's not in vain.

Student: Before the first stage of awakening, the stream-entry experience, are there places where a practitioner can experience the dropping away of the sense of self?

Luang Por Pasanno: Sure, wherever it arises! Just like any other conditioned phenomenon, the sense of self arises and passes away. It's just that we're so focused on the next thing that we don't notice the cessation.

Student: During the stream-entry experience, are the three lower fetters—personality view, attachment to practices and precepts, and skeptical doubt—all dropped at once, or in stages?

Luang Por Pasanno: All at once.

Student: Do the results of kamma speed up when you are practicing?

Luang Por Pasanno: Not necessarily. Kamma has its own way of playing itself out. There's a saying that kamma is going to do what kamma is going to do.

Student: The Buddha said that kamma can't be understood by a normal mind. Are there practitioners who have good enough concentration that they can understand parts of it?

Luang Por Pasanno: Oh, sure. There are meditators with good concentration who can see parts of it. But only the Buddha could understand it completely.

The Importance of
Informal Meditation

Ajahn Amaro • August 2008

Our teacher Ajahn Chah strongly discouraged us from holding a perception of meditation practice as different and apart from the activities of our ordinary everyday lives. There can be a tendency to think that meditation is what happens when we're walking up and down the meditation path or in the Dhamma Hall when we have our legs crossed and our eyes closed—that the rest is merely "the other stuff" we need to take care of so we can do "the real thing" of meditation. But Ajahn Chah was very keen to point out that we're capable of suffering in all modes of our lives, whether we're sitting on a cushion with our eyes closed, sitting in a classroom, working in the kitchen, driving down the freeway, or chatting with our friends. We can make difficulties for ourselves and experience happiness and unhappiness in every aspect of our lives. So it's important to bring all those different aspects of our lives into the scope of meditation.

Rather than thinking that meditation equals the activities in the hall or the walking path, it's more skillful to think in terms of "formal" and "informal" practice. When we sit with our eyes closed and legs crossed, that's formal practice. When working around the monastery and taking time with each other, this is the same practice, but in an informal mode. The informal practice is sometimes more challenging than sitting on our meditation cushions and trying to be mindful when everything is still, quiet, and highly controlled. So while we go about the various work tasks this morning, we can bring attention and mindfulness to them.

We can notice the different moods we're feeling. Are they exciting? *This is great. This is so wonderful!* Or are we thinking, *Oh no, another thing for me to fail at?* Maybe there's a feeling of pride. *My lines are straighter than anybody else's. Just look at these lines I painted!* The mind that creates problems can be very active. But with practice we're able to see through whatever state of mind happens to be in play.

We can watch the flow of moods, feelings, and thoughts as they go through the mind. We're not suppressing them or feeling that we shouldn't be experiencing these kinds of thoughts or attitudes, but neither are we buying into or being caught up in them. Instead, we're simply seeing that this is how the mind works. When things go well, we're happy. When things go badly, we're unhappy. That's just the way it is. We are recognizing that this is simply a flow of feeling and perception we're engaged in, noticing for example the different changes of the day. When we start the work period, it's nice, cool, and bright. *Ah, this is so lovely. What a beautiful place.* Then, when the temperature starts to pick up later in the morning, we might think, *Oh, it's really hot. It's only 10 o'clock, and I'm dying on my feet here.* We notice how our attitudes changed with the changing conditions. *Oh, how interesting. When it was cool, I felt happy. When it was hot, I felt oppressed. One is a feeling of comfort, the other is a feeling of discomfort.* We can see these as nothing more than different impressions and moods that come and go through the mind. We don't need to make a problem out of them.

By doing this, we're not negating anything, not thinking we shouldn't be feeling uncomfortable. We're merely seeing, *When it's like this I'm happy; when it's like that then I'm unhappy.* We see how fickle the mind can be, how easily we can get caught up in perceptions and moods. We simply bring mindfulness to that. The mind that's fully attentive to the present moment sees how easily we get caught up, and in that seeing there's a coolness of heart. There's an easefulness in the attitude. We find ourselves more easily able to go with the ups and downs of praise and criticism, success and failure, and with all the mundane, ordinary experiences that flow through the day.

Of course, applying this kind of attention and attitude isn't only for the morning work period, but for the entire course of the day. When the work period finishes, when we gather for the mealtime, after the meal is finished, when the dishes are done, and throughout our open time in the afternoon. We try to keep bringing our attention and the reflective attitude of mind to the flow of mood and perception. This is what's meant by "mindfulness of everyday life." It's as much a part of the meditation as is the formal, quiet sitting—perhaps even more so. The habit is to easily get caught up in the different conversations we're having or in the work we're engaged in so that we don't notice what's going on inside us. We're so busy and interested in active and external things. If we first apply a bit of attention to how we're feeling and attend a bit more closely to our attitude, this will help us find and retain a quality of balance and easefulness. We have the potential to be interested in what we are attending to, but it takes some effort to draw the attention inward.

These are some of the ways we learn to change the lens of our perceptions with regard to formal and informal meditation. Eventually, we may come to understand that meditation is an all-day and sometimes all-night activity. The more we are able to bring mindfulness and attention into every aspect of our lives, the more opportunities there are for wisdom and understanding to arise.

Like a Snake Shedding Its Skin

Ajahn Yatiko • May 2013

Many of us often live in a fog of time. We can become caught up in this fog—completely absorbed and obsessed with experiences that happened in the past or we hope will happen in the future. It's as if this perception of time has a reality to it that's independent of our own machinations and creations of the mind. But it's not separate, it's created and a part of our perception like everything else we experience. Sometimes we get entrapped and absorbed in it through the different physical and emotional difficulties we have, and we can't seem to rise above it.

But sometimes we *can* rise above it. Sometimes we can experience a clear perception of the present moment—the whole aspect of the mind that creates time through projection, memory, and hope. It is a vivid, here-and-now perception of what we're observing—like a portal, where we slip through the delusion of the created world we live in, and suddenly, we're in the present moment, which is grounded in reality and has a sense of authentic truth.

A metaphor comes to mind of a snake shedding its skin. The Buddha uses this image in the most profound sense, but I think it also applies to the present moment, where the snake's skin stands for time: this scaly, falsely created outer skin of delusion that's part of our own making. We move through it and leave it behind, which makes us naked and vulnerable. It's not vulnerable in the sense of being fragile or easily damaged. It's vulnerable in the sense of being able to receive the reality of the present moment—including everything we create in our minds—from a bare, new, and open field of awareness. It's freeing, liberating, lucid, and it has the quality of truth to it.

When we're caught up in our problems and locked into our difficulties and can't access the truthfulness of the present moment, we only have one option: patience. Sometimes we can't connect with the present moment because we're captivated by our actions and the results we're receiving from our actions. When that's the case, we have to be patient. There's nothing else we can do. Just because we cannot connect with the present moment doesn't mean we should give up on the Buddha's path and pack it in. We need to be patient and keep with the practice, reestablishing our wholesome intentions and our capacity for experiencing a present-moment awareness.

Spacious Practice

Ajahn Karuṇadhammo • June 2013

Having a sense of spaciousness is an important quality to look after in one's meditation practice. It's easy to become contracted and narrow in what we focus on, particularly during the work period when we can be quite involved with the task at hand. During this time we can easily remain involved, absorbed, enmeshed, and identified with the work we're doing. While intense focus like this can serve a purpose, the cultivation of an open and spacious mind can help keep this focus in the context of practice. This is talked about in certain meditation circles as keeping a "broad, choiceless awareness." It's a concept that is quite useful, but often misinterpreted. I've always appreciated Luang Por Pasanno's description of an unfocused spaciousness of mind as being "a nebulous nothingness that we are *not* trying to cultivate." We are not striving for *spaciness*, because *spaciousness* is different from that. This quality of space and being open carries with it a sense of alertness, attentiveness, and clear comprehension. Spaciousness doesn't mean that we drift, totally object-less—it's important we still maintain a frame of reference while we open up to that space.

This is quite a useful quality to cultivate. It's easy to get involved in our mental worlds but we can take the opportunity, even while working or walking from one place to another, to broaden the focus a bit. This helps to create a little more space in the mind and body without drifting off into an ethereal realm. It reminds me of something Ajahn Sumedho used to say, possibly quoting Ajahn Chah: "Oftentimes we think of the mind as being within the body. We have this body and inside it is the mind. But it may be even more skillful to consider that the body is in the mind." So with that broad, spacious, relaxed, open awareness we can keep the object of attention on the body itself, and see that the body is contained within that awareness. That's a good focus to maintain in the forest—walking up and down the trails, walking from one work site to another, or when we are doing anything using our bodies—we can tune into a relaxed, open, state of awareness. In this way we're not closed in on our mental worlds, but rather holding very clearly in our minds the object of the body moving through space. It may be a simple object, but it's one that keeps us tuned into the present moment, and helps us avoid the experience of drifting into spaciness.

This broadness of mind is also useful in sitting meditation—keeping the breath within that spacious context of an expansive awareness. We can pick up and cultivate any object within that spaciousness. For example, when cultivating the brahmavihāras—the qualities of loving-kindness, compassion, sympathetic joy, and equanimity, the states of mind that are talked about as boundless—we can establish that sense of an open and expansive mind, even before we start to pick up one of the brahmavihāras. That provides a broad, open container for the brahmavihāras where they can be developed. With any object we are developing, we can bring this spacious quality into our daily activities by establishing an open, easeful sense of the mind, and a broad awareness that is alert and attentive to what it is that is happening in the present moment.

Waiting Patiently Like a Tick

Luang Por Pasanno • May 2013

Recently I read an extensive article on ticks and Lyme disease. Entomologists use a technical term for what ticks do when they're sitting on leaves of grass, waiting. It's called "questing"—questing ticks. A tick waits patiently for an animal to come along. That's what they have to do: sit there and wait. I can remember often being with Ajahn Chah sitting and waiting. That's what we all do for much of our practice. On one level, we might think, *I need to do something.* But if we reframe it, we're simply sitting and questing—sitting and watching our breath, sitting and waiting for the meal to happen, sitting up at our kuṭis on our own. We can reframe how we hold these activities so that we are patient with the circumstances we're experiencing, rather than being prey to impulses and restless feelings that are so much a part of the human condition. We're constantly moving to do something, be something, get something, become something, accomplish something, or get rid of something. Instead, we can come back to a framework of patiently questing, deriving meaning and understanding from the experiences we have and the circumstances around us, rather than constantly trying to shift, move, and rearrange. So learn how to be patient like a sitting tick and use investigation so that it can be a real quest.

Working to Let Go

Ajahn Ñāṇiko • April 2013

The work period is a good time for learning about how to let go. During these periods the mind is constantly thinking, *I have to do this and I have to do that and this needs to get done before I do that.* But when the mind lets go, it's malleable and as the Buddha said, "fit for work." If we only meditate and don't challenge the mind with difficult and unpredictable situations, then the chances are the mind won't learn how to let go. What really trains us in how to let go are the uncertain situations we are faced with. We might tell ourselves, *Okay, today no matter what I do, no matter what anybody says to me, whether it's someone I don't like or someone I do, I'm going to let go no matter what.* And then, sure enough, as soon as we make that resolution, someone or something will come along and test us in a way we didn't think we would be tested, and we're unable to let go.

It's not only about letting go, it's also about choosing the appropriate response. We are training ourselves to respond judiciously and to let go within the bounds of a suitable response. By doing this we learn to maintain internal and external harmony.

If we learn how to let go during or after activity, the mind will not be stressed, and our default mental condition will be one of quietude. Then the mind will also be quiet when it does not need to work. When the mind needs to think or figure something out, it will do that and then go quiet again.

We do not need to stress out over external things which may seem important but in reality are insignificant. The external world is a mere trifle compared to our internal development. The work period, or any time we are doing something, is for seeking that internal development, for seeking the Dhamma, and for letting go.

Centering on a Clear, Still Place

Luang Por Pasanno • June 2005

Having a sense of centering, whether we're doing chores or sitting in meditation, can be a valuable practice for us. It's essential that we remember to center ourselves—to bring things to a central place—so that we're working from a still point, rather than having our energy and attention diffused and scattered out into the world around us. As we collect ourselves at that center point, it brings our energy together, and we're able to see things clearly, without adding in our likes and dislikes. Centering in this way provides us with a reliable place from which to reflect upon the Dhamma, a place from which to apply the teachings in our day-to-day lives.

Beginning With Good Habits

Ajahn Yatiko • June 2013

It is possible to have freedom from a mind that seems compulsively locked into habits and mind movements. We have the ability to completely put aside those habits and rest in a silent, quiet, spacious, aware, calm, and devotional place. The path that leads to this place is the path laid out by the Buddha—a transformative path releasing us from the habits of mind that cause us suffering.

As far as habits go, it's much easier to develop good habits right from the beginning rather than trying to correct our bad habits once they've set in. When people first come to live at a monastery— especially junior monks, novices, anagārikas, or long-term lay residents—that is the time for them to develop good habits. It's much easier to accomplish in the early years, because the energy to do so is most available and present. So that's the time to reflect on and establish the practices recommended by the Buddha.

Whenever we perform an action there's a tendency for that action to be repeated—that's an aspect of kamma. If we chose to act in a certain way under certain conditions, then whenever those conditions recur, we're likely to act in the same way. When new monastics often get caught up into busyness, distraction, and work projects, then it's likely they will continue getting caught up like that as time progresses. It will become their habit. Fortunately, this applies to our wholesome actions as well.

It is a great refuge for us to recollect that we've exerted a significant amount of effort in various aspects of the practice—study, meditation, different devotional practices, service, and other wholesome actions. This is a meaningful source of comfort, because we know that what we've done in the past is repeatable—we have established an ability to practice well. This can give us a sense of satisfaction, which is especially important when we're going through a difficult and challenging stretch. If I had never put forth effort in my early years, I think it would be very difficult for me to establish those wholesome habits for the first time now, because I wouldn't know I was capable of practicing in that way.

Challenging Our Perceptions of Work

Luang Por Pasanno • July 2013

It's helpful to consider and reflect on how we perceive work. If we bring up the word *work*, what comes to mind? There may be a feeling of drudgery, that it's onerous, maybe even odious, or a burden in some way. We often view work as something we're beset with, something we have to get done and out of the way before we can be comfortable and at ease. Or we may think of work as something that keeps us from our meditation practice. These are merely perceptions that come up in the mind, and it's helpful to challenge these perceptions.

If we do challenge them, we can learn to bring mindfulness into the work period, which helps us develop a continuity of attention and reflective clarity. When we approach the work period like this, we realize it isn't something to get out of the way, but rather, it's an important aspect of the training. We don't want to be like so many people who live their whole lives waiting for the work to be over: *When I get this done, I'll be happy, and I can relax* . . . and as death approaches, they're still waiting.

It's also helpful to remember that the work we do in the monastery serves to maintain the facilities here. We're looking after the places we live in for our own benefit, but also for the benefit of others. When we perceive our work in this way, we can recognize that it's an opportunity for giving, for generosity, and for putting forth effort that benefits everyone. These are opportunities to do something quite noble. We're reminded that generosity is not limited to material things, but includes acts of service—wholesome, skillful, and selfless actions. As a result, our work can become a source of well-being and happiness.

In Thai, the word for *work* also means festival. This blurs the distinction between work and enjoyment. If it's a festival, it's an opportunity to get together and have a good time. This creates a completely different perception than drudgery. During my time in Thailand, I was always struck by the northeastern villagers who came to the monastery to work. They really enjoyed themselves. They saw this work as an opportunity to do good things together. We can take a page from their book and use work as an opportunity to develop a sense of lightness within the mind—learning to enjoy work as generous and beneficial.

The Power of Speech

Ajahn Karuṇadhammo • October 2013

I was thinking about an aspect of our practice, right speech, and reflecting on the power of speech to affect us all. In some ways it affects us even more than bodily actions, which we think of as the coarsest way of acting out a mental condition. Speech can have an even broader effect because the number of people who can hear spoken words is greater than the number of people who can observe somebody's bodily action. Knowing how powerful it is, we need to put a great amount of care and attention into our speech because it can impact each one of us for better or for worse, depending on what is said. I believe that many of us here have a keen intellect with well-developed mental faculties, as well as the ability to rationalize and this often results in having some fairly strong views and opinions. I see that in myself. If we combine that with the ability to articulate, and to put those ideas, thoughts, and intellectual capacities into speech, then the outcome is that one has an extremely powerful tool. It is helpful for us to recognize this power and the possibility of its ramifications.

Thinking historically, we see how one person in this past century, with a strong intellect and a powerful ability to articulate, influenced an entire culture to the point that, even though he may not have personally taken many lives himself, he was responsible for the destruction of six million Jews and millions of other people. He also justified horrible kinds of experimentation on human beings. All of this took place simply because of the power of his intellect and speech.

Conversely, speech can be used on a mass scale for good. We realize this when we look at our own teacher, the Buddha, who was able to use speech for the benefit of many, many people. And 2,600 years later, his ability to communicate and use speech effectively has continued to have a strong influence worldwide.

For better or for worse, speech can be an exceptionally powerful tool and here in our community, we need to be aware that it can have a potent and long-lasting effect. If we have a keen ability to think, rationalize, and analyze, as well as the ability to articulate, it doesn't mean that our speech is always free from defilement. With all of those qualities the underlying negative tendencies can still be expressed. Sometimes we may feel a need to prove something or to be correct, or feel that something must be done in a certain way, or try to position ourselves within the community in a way that is promoting our views. Those kinds of tendencies are an indication that we are not completely free of basic animal instincts. Our brains may have well-developed cortices and speech centers but we also have the lower functioning parts that are influenced by basic unwholesome tendencies toward territory, ownership, and a sense of "me" and "mine." These tendencies are still part of our cultural inheritance, our kamma, and our biology. No matter how skilled we are with an ability to speak, no matter how clever we are in the way we think and analyze, these tendencies still come bubbling up.

We need to be aware of that and use our speech in a way that is conducive to harmony, because we also have the ability to harmonize. Think about how powerful and uplifting it can be when there is a discussion in the community centered on Dhamma. Similarly, somebody may express intentions toward kindness, support, clarification, and truth by articulating a harmonious viewpoint, something that contributes to the welfare and well-being of the community. We can develop harmonious speech by using the skills we have learned practicing the Dhamma to check our speech when kamma starts to bubble up. If a conversation is heading in the wrong direction, then one needs to be able to stop it, change direction, or skillfully withdraw if necessary. We can then move toward establishing speech that is not only well expressed but also grounded in kindness and an interest in supporting the welfare of the whole community.

Choosing Contention or Contentment

Ajahn Amaro • December 2008

On the winter solstice I led a daylong retreat at Spirit Rock with the theme, "Maximum Darkness." We investigated the experiences of death, loss, and sadness. It was a suitably dingy, gray, wet day, appropriate to that dolorous subject. For many years, one of the exercises I used in my meditation—and a theme I had others use on this daylong retreat—was to imagine the current sitting I was doing to be the last minutes of my life. When we did this together for the day, I didn't let the others know how long the sitting was going to be—ten minutes, twenty minutes, half an hour—so that we could really focus on each breath, each moment, as if it were the last moment of our lives.

I encouraged the participants to reflect, *If this truly were the last few minutes of my life, then what happens to my priority list?* If we take seriously that the bell is the last moment, then consider what's important and see what comes up in the mind with all of those things to do, the anxieties about going to the dentist, and so on. Just reflect on that, *How do I relate to the things I've left half done, the things I'm so proud of, the things I regret?*

I've found this theme very useful, and for years when I was at Chithurst Monastery I would make it a daily practice. Luang Por Sumedho would always be the one ringing the bell at the end of the sittings, and at the beginning I would imagine, *Okay, this is the last forty-five minutes or last hour of my life. What will my mind be dwelling on when the bell is rung? Can I drop it and be ready to go by the time the sound of the ringing fades?* It's often quite shocking, the kind of things that the mind is obsessed about or focused on. So we can ask ourselves, *Would I really want to be thinking of this or dwelling on that at the time of death?* That reflection then allows us to develop the capacity to drop things, to let go.

One woman at the daylong retreat saw a dichotomy in her mind, she saw a certain choice. The choice was between contention and contentment. What took shape in her mind was a clear distinction between being "content with" the way things are, or "contending against" the way things are. I thought it was quite insightful and interesting how her mind had produced that way of formulating the dichotomy. She authentically summarized the choice we all have at any moment during the day. Working out in the cold with the rain dripping down our necks, carrying large uncomfortable objects across slippery mud and not wanting to drop them, finding places to store 300 apples and oranges in a confined space, whatever it might be, we have the capacity to *contend against*, and we have the capacity to be *content with*—to attune ourselves with the way things are as we go about our tasks. It's a choice.

Often we relate to obstacles in our lives as being unavoidable. It's as if they've been put in our way deliberately, and we feel burdened and frustrated by them. These are qualities of resentment and negativity, desires to avoid or to switch off. But it's important to recognize that even if something is particularly obstructive—carrying a large clumsy object across slippery wet clay in the rain—it's up to us whether we tense up about it and contend against it. It's our choice to buy into our story and contend against the way things are, becoming anxious or irritated—or not. This is a theme I often use for my own practice, to recognize, *It's my choice whether I make a problem out of this, or not. It's my choice to be content with this—or not.*

Our application of mindfulness and clear comprehension, *sati* and *sampajañña*, has a lot to do with recognizing that we have choices in how we react to the world around us and to our internal states of mind. If we also apply the quality of wisdom or discernment, *paññā*, then we will choose the path of non-contention, of cultivating the capacity to attune. Even in the midst of the most difficult or challenging circumstances, we don't have to dwell in aversion, we don't have to contend against these circumstances. We can find a quality of peace and clarity in relationship to every situation, even those we would not choose. We begin to see that there's nothing in life that is inherently obstructive or unsatisfactory. It all hinges on the way we choose to handle it.

The Paradox of Urgency

Luang Por Pasanno • October 2013

We may feel there exists a paradox or inconsistency having to do with some of the teachings that guide our spiritual practice and how we conduct our daily lives. First we're told it's important to have a sense of urgency, and then we're told to relax, let go, and cultivate a feeling of spaciousness.

On one side, the Buddha encourages us to cultivate the quality of *saṃvega*, which is usually translated as a sense of spiritual urgency. It's the recognition that life is short and everything is uncertain, so we need to take this practice seriously. We urgently need to apply our attention and effort in order to fulfill the teachings and not miss out on the opportunity we have.

On the other side, we need to learn how to relax and not get caught up in the feeling of urgency. We tend to pile stuff onto ourselves, thinking, *I have to get this done and that done.* Or we might feel an urgency with regard to future planning, *We have to have a budget meeting, and we have to have an insurance meeting, and we have to have a business meeting, and ...* This agitating sort of urgency can arise not only with our chores and duties, but with our internal spiritual practice as well, *I have to get my mindfulness of breathing straight, and I have to keep my reflections going, and ...* With this sense of urgency in trying to do everything all at once, we end up becoming frantic and, ironically, very little gets done well or efficiently—it really doesn't work.

So instead we can remind ourselves, *Hey, it's just one thing at a time, one moment at a time, one breath at a time.* We can learn to create some space for ourselves and not carry the "I have to" tendency around with us, nor the impulse that tells us that everything is so urgent.

As we reflect on these seemingly paradoxical qualities of urgency and spaciousness, we may find that they are not inconsistent after all. We can apply both of them in our practice, with a sense of balance, emphasizing one or the other depending on the circumstances. In doing so, we need to come from a place of clarity and steadiness. Clarity is needed to anchor spaciousness and letting go, and to guide those actions that arise out of a sense of urgency. Steadiness is needed to bring good results from those actions, and to keep spaciousness from turning into spacing out. This place of clarity and steadiness is where paradoxes like these dissolve and fade away.

Tuning Into Your Conscience

Ajahn Yatiko • April 2013

There's a certain danger that may arise when we listen to these reflections every day. For those of us who are community residents—who are here all the time and have listened to these reflections every day for years—the danger is that we might develop an attitude whereby we think, *The senior monk is just doing his thing, giving a reflection, and it doesn't really affect me. I don't need to pay attention or internalize any of it. Here's my chance to zone out and think about something else.*

If that is our experience then it's a real loss, because the purpose of these reflections is to help create the conditions for all of us to practice and positively influence the atmosphere of the monastery in some way. Some reflections may include information or a practical reminder, but the essential purpose, motivation, and intention is to provide a form of communication and energy that's going to uplift, encourage, and support the community.

As an encouragement today, I'd like each of us to tune into our own situations. On some level we're the ones who know what needs to be said and what we need to hear. Spend a couple of minutes in silence tuning into your conscience and asking yourself, *What is it that I need to hear? What is a good thing for me to hear? What kind of reflection is really appropriate to my situation now?* The purpose is not to make us comfortable and happy. Rather, it's to foster an understanding from which we can say to ourselves, *Truly, this is what I need. This is what's going to be good for me and my practice.* So spend a few minutes imagining what that reflection might be. This requires sensitivity—a tuning into the conscience. Please, take a few minutes for that.

Putting Our Moods in Their Place

Luang Por Pasanno • July 2013

I've been thinking about Ajahn Ñāṇadhammo, recalling his most memorable interaction with Ajahn Chah while living at Wat Pah Pong.

One day while out on alms round, Ajahn Ñāṇadhammo had a slight argument with another monk and became stirred up and upset. When he returned to the monastery, Ajahn Chah smiled at him and uncharacteristically in English said, "Good morning." Of course Ajahn Ñāṇadhammo was really tickled with that, and this feeling of happiness arose that was uplifting for him.

In the late afternoon, he went over to Ajahn Chah's dwelling place. Oftentimes monks would go over there in the afternoon when laypeople came by to pay respects and ask questions; it was a good opportunity to hear Ajahn Chah give advice. As evening approached, Ajahn Chah sent everybody off to *pūjā*, except for Ajahn Ñāṇadhammo, who alone was asked to stay. He sat beneath Luang Por Chah, massaging his feet. In the distance he could hear the chanting of evening pūjā, with the stillness of the forest almost palpable. Ajahn Ñāṇadhammo described it as an ethereal, heavenly experience, and he felt quite blissful.

Suddenly, Ajahn Chah pulled his foot away and kicked Ajahn Ñāṇadhammo in the chest, sending him flat on his back. This was quite a shock, of course. Then Ajahn Chah said,

"You're not really paying attention to the practice or the training. You have an argument in the morning and get upset, carrying around a mood of ill will. Then all it takes is one person to say good morning to you, and you go off into a happy mood, spending the day proliferating about that. You come over here and even more happens that pleases you, so you get into an even happier mood. Next I put you flat on your back, and you're confused. That's not the mind of a practitioner, that's not the mind of somebody who is training in Dhamma. You have to be able to stop yourself from following your moods. You do your best not to be caught by them, believe in them, or buy into them. That's what defines a practitioner." As one might imagine, this was an exceedingly powerful and influential teaching for Ajahn Ñāṇadhammo.

For all of us, moods are woven into the fabric of our lives. We go up and down, get inspired and depressed, energetic or enervated by our moods. None of that is the essence of practice. To really practice is to see through these conditions, to see them clearly, as they really are, *This is just a mood. This happens to be something I like. This happens to be something I dislike.* It doesn't mean we don't have feelings, but we resist picking them up and running with them all the time.

As we go about our day, we need to look at the nature of our impressions—to look at the contact, the feelings, and the way moods want us to go—and stop ourselves from giving in to them. We have to be willing to look closely at moods and challenge them. With peaceful moods, for instance, if we get what we want and things go the way we prefer, that's not very stable, that's no refuge at all. The refuge is in *sati-paññā*—mindfulness and wisdom. We use sati-paññā to cultivate truth-discerning awareness at all times. We know our moods, we know their arising and their fading away. Whether they are pleasant or unpleasant, we don't get caught by them nor do we follow them. We learn to relinquish this tendency of mind.

Deconstructing Personas

Ajahn Karuṇadhammo • August 2013

Recently I've been reflecting on the ways we project ourselves to the world, and the relief that comes when we set these projections down. Many of us feel the need to constantly create a persona based on either how we think we should be, or how we want others to view us. If we can get an idea of how that process occurs, then we have the potential to catch it in its tracks. By noticing this fabrication before it becomes too involved or too set in, we're able to use reflection to let it deconstruct. The less we try to create a sense of who we are, or who we want people to see us as, then the more natural and at ease we can be.

Earlier I suggested seeing if walking meditation could be used as a reflection—walking back and forth with the thought in mind, *I don't have to be anybody right now.* By doing this for a short period of time, we are planting the seed that may help us stop creating an identity to present to the world. Instead of forming that identity, we simply see, if even for a finger snap, what it's like to no longer create that image in our minds.

When there is a period where we don't need to think too hard—moving from one place to another in a moment of transition or simply getting up to go to the bathroom during the work period—whatever mundane activity it may be, we can notice this. We can ask ourselves, *Can I drop this created image of being somebody who's operating in the world? Could I at least notice whether or not I'm holding this perception of a person who behaves in a certain way—with a role, a purpose, an image or projection of a solid independent individual?* Then try to let go of that created self-image for just a moment, see what it might feel like. Feel the sense of relief and ease that arises when it's simply a few body parts and a few stray thoughts moving through space and time.

The Triple Gem Is the Middle Way

Ajahn Yatiko • August 2013

It's interesting how things change when Luang Por Pasanno leaves. Suddenly the energy in the community shifts. When a senior monk is the head of a community, one of his roles is to figuratively place himself into the center of that community. From that central point, he provides a focus for the community that is both encouraging and inspiring for those members. His role is part of the external world we live in here. But we each occupy an internal world as well, and each of us is at the center of that world. And from that center, when push comes to shove, we're each responsible for our own inspiration, encouragement, and well-being.

So we have to find a way of centering ourselves that doesn't depend on some person of authority or other external form of support—to find a center that can serve as a point of focus and a stable refuge. If we take our own desires and selfish cravings as a refuge, that's a recipe for suffering. When we do that, we're headed toward an empty, dead-ended, self-centered solitude that's very painful to experience. On the other extreme, we could place the external world at our center, seeking refuge in trying to serve and help, focusing all of our energies on those in need. But one of the cold, hard facts of this world is that there are many more beings in need than we could possibly help in a meaningful way. Trying to center ourselves in unreserved, unremitting service often leads to suffering, frustration, and burnout.

The Middle Way for all of this—for finding a center—is based on the Triple Gem—the Buddha, the Dhamma, and the Saṅgha. We can rely on the Triple Gem for our center. We already know how much time we waste focused on our own little thoughts, ideas, perceptions, aspirations, hopes, and anxieties. We can get out of that mode by calling to mind the Triple Gem—something extra-mundane and transcendent. We can let our internal worlds revolve around and focus on that. When we focus on the Triple Gem as our center, the focus is neither on ourselves nor on other people, yet it is something that radiates everywhere, toward all beings, including ourselves. Although maintaining this center requires effort, we need not depend on external people or conditions to make it happen.

Using the Breath to Balance the Mind

Luang Por Pasanno • April 2013

It has been nine days since we ended our three-month retreat, which seems like a good time to remind everyone: Don't forget to connect with mindfulness of the body and mindfulness of the breath. With the body, use the simple rhythms of moving from one place to another. Attend to that. Make it an anchor for developing mindfulness and awareness.

As for the breath, Ajahn Chah would often say, "People complain that they don't have time to meditate, but do they have time to breathe?" Well, of course we have time to breathe. But if we don't direct our attention to our breathing, then our attention slides by, and we end up absorbed in proliferation, expectation, irritation, or whatever. So we must remember to consciously bring attention to the breath. Then we can learn how to *use* the breath.

To begin, notice that breathing in has a different effect on the mind and body than breathing out. When we breathe in, there's an expansion of the body—we are bringing in the life force, expanding and energizing what one might call the system of our existence. That's different from breathing out, which is a release, a settling, a stopping. These distinct qualities have different effects on the mind. By knowing that and by paying close attention to what's happening, we can use the different effects of our in-breaths and out-breaths to work with the mind when it's out of balance.

For instance, if the mind is leaning toward dullness and wanting not to deal with things, we can consciously attend to the in-breath and the energy it brings—enlivening, expanding, and brightening the mind. At other times, the mind may be leaning toward distraction, doing, and becoming. Then we need to pay more attention to the out-breath, allowing the mind to settle down. By working with the breath in such ways, we can balance the mind, attuning ourselves with each in-breath and out-breath.

When we engage in any activity, whether sitting in front of a computer or out on the trail with a rake, we are still breathing, still occupying a physical body within the world around us. Each activity is an opportunity to inquire of ourselves, *Where is my attention going? Am I aware of the body, of my in-breaths and out-breaths? What is needed to find a place of balance and clarity? Does the mind need lifting up, or settling down?* By doing this, we are caring for our practice throughout the day, not just during morning and evening meditation. We are developing the continuity of practice that is needed for the most beneficial results.

Noticing When Heat Arises

Ajahn Amaro • December 2008

It often strikes me how the Fire Sermon is the shortest of the three cardinal discourses of the Buddha, taking less than fifteen minutes to chant. Yet during the course of the Buddha's teaching it, a thousand *bhikkhus* became *arahants*, enlightened beings no longer subject to rebirth. In the Pāli Canon that's the largest number of people who were completely liberated during the course of listening to a single Dhamma talk. It's a powerful teaching, although it can seem unremarkable in certain ways.

In the sutta, the Buddha goes through a list explaining how all of the aspects of the senses are burning with greed, hatred, and delusion. The eye, eye consciousness, eye contact, the feeling that arises with eye contact, visual objects, everything to do with the process of vision—and the same with the processes of hearing, smelling, tasting, touching, and mental activities— they're all burning with passion, aversion, and delusion. He then says, "*Evaṃ passaṃ bhikkhave sutvā ariyasāvako cakkhusmiṃ pi nibbindati ...*—Seeing thus, bhikkhus, the wise noble disciple becomes dispassionate toward the eye, toward visual objects, toward eye consciousness, toward eye contact, and the feeling that arises with eye contact," and so on through the remaining five senses.

It's extraordinarily simple and direct. First, seeing that the senses are on fire; second, recognizing that they're on fire, agitated, heated; and then third, responding with coolness, *nibbindati*, dispassion. *Nibbidā* is related to *Nibbāna*, coolness—there's a cooling in relationship to the senses. And with that cooling down, that dispassion, the hearts of those thousand bhikkhus were liberated. It's extraordinarily simple. In the sutta, it almost seems as if nothing has happened, as if very little instruction was given. But like many other Buddhist teachings, particularly in the Pāli tradition, if we blink, we miss it. The teachings can be quite subtle. They're not very demonstrative or highly elaborate. This particular teaching is like that. We can easily miss the key piece: having the mindfulness to recognize—to recognize the quality of burning, to recognize that things are agitated and heated, to recognize the friction around what we see, smell, taste, hear, touch, and think.

During the course of the day, it's helpful to recognize with mindfulness that quality of friction or tension—what the Buddha calls heat, *āditta*, burning. The feeling can be one of ownership regarding some tool, the interest in a particular task, or the irritation with an exceptionally obstructive piece of rock that won't move out of the way. Whatever it might be—some computer program or printer that won't obey—whether aversion, delusion, or passion, it can be extremely subtle and thus hard to recognize. It can also be obvious, gross, and clearly visible—but even so, there's no guarantee we'll recognize it. Recognition requires mindfulness.

As we bring mindfulness to the course of our days, we can observe the sense world and how we respond to what we see, hear, smell, taste, touch, and think—the mental realms of moods, memories, ideas, and plans. We can notice when that heat arises. We notice the heat of *rāga*, of passion, wanting, and desiring; the heat of *dosa*, of aversion, being irritated, upset, obstructed; the heat of *moha*, delusion, caught up in reactions, opinions, assumptions, projections, and other deluded states. These are all aspects of heat in the context of this teaching.

By practicing with that quality of mindfulness—*evaṃ passaṃ*, seeing thus—we're able to recognize a feeling of ownership, for example. We can recognize the heat that the mind generates out of simple things. *Oh look, I'm getting upset with this machine, I'm getting excited about this plan I have, I'm claiming this painting project as mine.* A task we didn't even know existed before it was assigned to us, suddenly becomes "mine." *I hope no one sees that awful wood cut I made.* "Look, that cut's not square and we all know who did it!" *That would be so embarrassing.* By owning something, it can become our great achievement or our terrible crime—the heat of pride or the heat of shame. So again, "*Evaṃ passaṃ bhikkhave sutvā ariyasāvako . . . pi nibbindati*—Seeing thus, bhikkhus, the wise noble disciple becomes dispassionate . . ."

We can see how the mind creates these stupid, absurd reactions and projections about the world, and at the same time, what an amazing, wonderful capacity we have to cool down, let go, and not create heat around these things. "The wise, noble disciple becomes dispassionate toward the eye, ear, nose, tongue, body, and mind." Even though that's a subtle teaching in some ways, it's also incredibly essential and helpful. When we take the opportunity to cool down, to let the fire go out, then lo and behold, life becomes much easier, more pleasant, and open. There's less heat, friction, and abrasion in our world.

The Mango Picking Pole Is Too Long

Luang Por Pasanno • August 2013

Sometimes we feel compelled to think, figure things out, analyze what we're doing, and marshal all the logical reasons for directing our practice in a particular way, but in the end, it's simply busyness. And an important part of our practice is developing skills that prevent the mind from being trapped in busyness.

Ajahn Chah used the example of picking mangoes. In Thailand, mangoes are picked by using a long bamboo pole with a little basket at the end. Usually the mangoes are on branches fifteen or twenty feet from the ground. Ajahn Chah would say, "If our mango pole is twenty-five or thirty feet, it is much too long for the task. When considering what things could advance our practice, we might think having a Ph.D. or being really smart would help. But that may be like having too long of a pole: too much thinking, too much intelligence, too much of figuring things out. It may not be what is needed."

We do need to use reflection and investigation to understand our experiences. But that reflection and investigation needs to be appropriate and balanced. In the same way that picking mangoes requires a pole that's been cut to the proper length, we need to tailor our thought processes to the task at hand. The task at hand is understanding: *How do I not suffer? How do I not create problems? How do I not increase my suffering and confusion?* Those questions are more important than, *Do I have all the information I need? Should I think more about my problem? What logic can I use to figure it out?* This can be mental overkill—more than what the Buddha would have us do.

Instead, we can learn to maintain a balance in our use of thinking and logical analysis. We do this by paying close attention to what is useful in helping us prevent or ease suffering and confusion. We can learn to apply thought at the right time and in the right amount, and learn how to let go of thought when it's not necessary.

I Can Hardly Wait

Ajahn Yatiko • April 2013

I was at the Island Hermitage in Sri Lanka this past winter, where it was very beautiful. While there, I did a fair amount of contemplation around the topic of illness, which I found very useful to my practice. The Buddha recommends this contemplation as one of the subjects for recollection: *I am of the nature to sicken; I have not gone beyond sickness.* While on my walking path I would bring it to mind: *This is going to happen to me, there's no question about it. Sickness is going to come upon me and most importantly, pain is going to come upon me.* This sort of reflection isn't meant to be depressing or to increase anxiety. It simply functions as a means of facing an existential truth.

Here at Abhayagiri, we might be walking up and down on our walking path on a beautiful day. It could be 75 degrees, the flowers are out, and we feel strong and bright. Times like these are especially good for reflecting that illness is coming and at some point we will experience great pain. Rather than treating the matter in an abstract way, it's best to be realistic, asking ourselves, *What does it mean that this body is subject to pain? How am I going to prepare for that? What does it mean that pain is going to come upon this body?*

This kind of reflection is valuable for several reasons. When we reflect like this, it is possible for the superficial things that preoccupy the mind to fade away into the background. It feels quite liberating to be mindful that pain or death will be experienced. That awareness itself fosters a sense of readiness for the time when pain eventually does come to the body. We can also use this practice when illness or pain is actually present within us.

If we use our intelligence and think too much, it can lead to intellectual endeavors that are not helpful. Truly, what we want to cultivate is the mindfulness and awareness that can help us recognize that, *This body is not who I am. This body is subject to many experiences—feelings, pain of all sorts, and death.* If we are mindful, this reflection can be uplifting—we recognize that we are facing something that is the truth of the condition in which we are living. It helps us feel much more familiar and intimate with these realities and therefore, less afraid of them.

When Luang Por Sumedho was once asked how he feels about death, he grinned and responded, "I can hardly wait." I can relate to that. Once we truly accept death we can simply see it as a fascinating transformation, as a great change that will come upon us. That is all that is happening, nothing more. We are moving into the space of a total unknown, and it is going to be a radical transformation. That's exciting and interesting, to say the least. Admittedly, death is uncertain, so we don't want to slip into superstition or ungrounded confidence with regard to it. We simply want to be willing to open ourselves to it, to trust in the kamma we have made as human beings and especially, as Buddhist practitioners. By trusting in that kamma, we can have the courage to open up to the uncertainty of what will come. That is the real adventure of the death process.

We are all involved in this project together. There is no project more important than deeply coming to terms with, and understanding, our condition as beings who are subject to birth, aging, illness, and ultimately, death. Everything else is far down the list.

Making Uncertainty Clear

Luang Por Pasanno • June 2013

I received an e-mail the other day from Ajahn Ñāṇiko and Tan Ṭhitābho, who recently left on their *tudong* from here to Oregon. They had arrived safely at Steve's place in Willits and were camped out on the floor of his shrine room, sore and aching because it was their first day of walking. They weren't used to carrying all their gear for such a long distance, but they'll get used to it. They were planning to leave Willits yesterday and head up north. Who knows how far they might get today and where they'll be going on alms round. That is part of the adventure and part of the practice of taking on uncertainty, *anicca*.

When we are out on the road walking like that, uncertainty is a constant presence. In fact, wherever we are and whatever we are doing—whether on tudong, walking back to our hut, or working on a project—uncertainty is a constant companion. But often we don't acknowledge its presence. We tend to fall into assumptions of certainty, assumptions that this is a sure thing or this is going to be a certain way. We assume that everything is laid out clearly, such as how our day is going to go, who will be here, and what can happen. There is, of course, a certain fallacy to those assumptions. It is important to remind ourselves of the uncertainty of our existence, the uncertainty of what is happening around us, and the uncertainty of the things we rely on for comfort, security, and well-being. As a part of practice and training, it is essential to keep bringing up the reflection of impermanence.

When the Buddha speaks about the universal characteristics of all phenomena, anicca is the very first quality he points to. In many suttas, the Buddha expresses that it is essential to bring awareness to the truth of impermanence. When we bring awareness to the truth that everything is changing, it doesn't make us more anxious or fearful. Rather, it brings a sense of clarity and immediacy. But uncertainty and change are often not engaged with, and so they slip into the background. When something is in the background, it tends to be fuzzy and imperceptible, and we can have all sorts of incorrect assumptions about it.

Aniccā vatta saṅkhāra—all conditioned things, all phenomena, are impermanent—that phrase begins one of the suttas in the Dhammapada. By making an effort to bring to mind this reflection on uncertainty and change, we have an opportunity to brighten and clarify the mind with the truth of impermanence, the truth of our conditioned experience.

A Lifetime of Maintenance

Ajahn Karuṇadhammo • November 2013

I was looking around the monastery thinking about the tasks that we have today. I'm going to be working with a couple of other people checking out our septic system, seeing what's going in and whether it is working properly. We're also cleaning up different areas around the cloister. As I was looking down at the cloister construction site, I saw dug-out earth, cement, and rebar forming the foundation of what in the future will be our reception hall building.

I was reflecting on the fact that people don't often think about, see, or experience the underside of the monastery—the buildings, operations, functions, and infrastructure. When we look at a building that's completely built, like the monks utility building, we don't automatically visualize or see the foundation, the earthwork, or the dug-out area. We see the building itself that's structured on top of it. When we're eating, washing dishes, and putting our bowls away, we don't usually visualize the food that we eat eventually coming out of our bodies and going into the septic system. There's the starting of different projects and repairs, but we don't usually pay attention to them once they've been completed. In thinking about the beginnings and endings of these kinds of processes, what is it that we choose to experience? We view the world from what's on the surface and what is most pleasing to the eye. We selectively attune to that aspect of an experience because that's what we want to see. It's naturally how we live our lives.

For the most part, we do what we need to do to get through the day, but we don't pay attention to the aspects of existence that are unpleasant, unexciting, unattractive, tedious, routine, or mundane. We're usually working and living our lives in a way that's trying to get through the unpleasant and boring events, while at the same time looking forward to the pleasant bits—"the good stuff."

As we are practicing, it can be helpful to pay attention to all of the routine maintenance and tedious tasks that we engage in, from the beginning of the day to the end of the day. Whether it's the areas where we live, the physical surroundings, our bodies, our minds, or the relationships we have with people—we are consistently maintaining these structures. We tend to miss or skip over that whole aspect of our daily lives— the routine maintenance. If we miss it, then it's as if we are walking through a cloud. There is the intention of experiencing the one or two moments that are exceptionally interesting, exciting, or pleasurable, but the rest of it is just a cloud. With exception to the rare high and low spots, 90 percent of our lives are the routine, "in-between" experiences. But if we can bring mindfulness to the routine and mundane aspects of the day and not be so caught up in doing something to get somewhere exciting in the future, then there's a lot more peace and ease of mind and less desire momentum propelling us. We can settle back into a recognition of simply being here right now with whatever our experience is. This is the most pleasant and peaceful abiding we can have.

An Internal Articulation of Dhamma

Luang Por Pasanno • July 2012

I've been noticing something in my speech that I find irritating. It's my use of filler words such as "like, sort of, um." I think to myself, *Am I getting more and more inarticulate and hopeless with age?* Then I listen to other people, and it's pretty much the same. To break that habit, we can learn to internally compose what we want to say before we speak, rather than fumbling around with "um, ah, sort of, like, er."

Even worse is the tendency to use speech that is imprecise. This is particularly problematic when it comes to speaking about the Dhamma. Being imprecise about the Dhamma does not benefit the Dhamma. The Dhamma itself is extremely clear, and we should reflect that clarity in our speech. Again, one way to do that is by focusing internally on what we're about to say before we say it. Not only will this help us compose our thoughts so they are clear, it will also help us uncover any defects that exist in our understanding.

We can encourage ourselves or even encourage each other—if people are open to it—to highlight our speech patterns as a tool for clarifying our own thoughts and for seeing how we express and communicate our ideas to others. The benefit is that internal clarity arises as well as the internal articulation of Dhamma.

The Importance of Worldly Discretion

Ajahn Jotipālo • July 2013

One word mentioned in the Mettā Sutta is *nipako*. It is often translated as wise, chief, or highest. Bhikkhu Bodhi translates it as discretion and talks about it in terms of worldly skills or practical wisdom. One way to reflect on this translation of nipako is in the realm of human relationships. By looking back on a conversation, for instance, we can ask ourselves whether we had been gentle and appropriate in that situation, and whether we had been deliberately paying attention to the quality of our speech at that time. In this way we can hone our communication skills and learn how to live more harmoniously in community. When we get upset or are involved in a misunderstanding or miscommunication, this word nipako points to how we can use discretion and practical wisdom with this type of experience. We can learn how to skillfully approach a person and work out a problem even in a situation that is difficult or uncomfortable.

Nipako comes from the root word *nipa*, which means to lay low. So I think of it as not jumping into a conversation with the first thing that comes to mind, and not trying to be the first person to come up with a quick solution. Instead, it is more akin to paying attention and watching.

We can also think of nipako in terms of learning and seeking guidance. For example, it's important to take the time to learn how things work instead of jumping in and trying to fix some particular thing when we really don't know how. Otherwise, we might damage what ever it is and create a bigger problem in the long run. We need to learn to ask for guidance. This applies to meditation as well. It's good to try new approaches and explore different techniques on our own, but it's also good to ask and seek advice from those with wisdom.

So with this quality of nipako we can apply our discretion and worldly skills in all situations. We can learn to lay low with circumspection, while learning from those who know what we don't. These are all qualities highly commended by the Buddha.

Renunciation: Not a Simple Matter

Ajahn Yatiko • August 2012

Renunciation is a lovely reflection to bring up from time to time. Sometimes people talk about how they've renounced something they were strongly attached to. They say that having renounced it, they're now done with it, once and for all. However, it's rarely as simple as that. Being attached to something means we don't want to let it go. If we recognize that something is harmful, a desire may arise to let it go, but we may still have a difficult time doing so. Attachment and renunciation are a pair, and their relationship can be complicated, so it's good to reflect on them both equally. When we're attached to something, simply making a decision to renounce it doesn't mean we're done. It's a process.

Letting go from the heart takes passion, questing, searching, determination, time, and cultivating the right kamma. Renunciation is something that requires commitment, time, and patience. It takes every opportunity we have to incline the mind toward letting things go. But we can start with small steps, letting go of little problems and complications. In doing so, we find that in time, we're making headway on the bigger issues we struggle with; letting go of the smaller problems and attachments eventually leads to letting go of the bigger ones. We learn to let go where we can, renounce where we can and as a result, find peace where we can.

Challenging Our Perceptions of Work

Luang Por Pasanno • July 2013

It's helpful to consider and reflect on how we perceive work. If we bring up the word *work*, what comes to mind? There may be a feeling of drudgery, that it's onerous, maybe even odious. We often view work as something we're beset with, something we have to get done and out of the way before we can be comfortable and at ease. Or we may think of work as something that keeps us from our meditation practice. These are merely perceptions that come up in the mind, and it's helpful to challenge them.

If we do challenge them, we can learn to bring mindfulness into the work period, which helps us develop a continuity of attention and reflective clarity. When we approach the work period like this, we realize it isn't something to get out of the way, but rather, it's an important aspect of the training. We don't want to be like so many people who live their whole lives waiting for the work to be over: *When I get this done, I'll be happy and I can relax* ... and as death approaches, they're still waiting.

It's also helpful to remember that the work we do in the monastery serves to maintain the facilities here. We're looking after the places we live in for our own benefit and for the benefit of others. When we perceive our work in this way, we can recognize that it's an opportunity for giving, for generosity, and for putting forth effort that benefits everyone. We're reminded that generosity is not limited to material things, but includes acts of service, wholesome, skillful, and selfless actions. As a result, our work can become a source of well-being and happiness.

In Thai, the word for *work* also means festival. This blurs the distinction between work and enjoyment. During my time in Thailand, I was always struck by the northeastern villagers who came to the monastery to work. They really enjoyed themselves. They saw this work as an opportunity to do good things together. We can take a page from their book and use our work as an opportunity to develop a sense of lightness, to enjoy pitching in together and enjoy doing what is beneficial.

Seeing Clearly Into the Chain of Causation

Ajahn Amaro • August 2005

Last week at the Spirit Rock Family Retreat, we saw many small, young, human beings surrounded by wholesome structures and examples offered in the way of skillful guidance. Seeing the good results of that in just a few days made me reflect on the idea that if we can catch things early and have an influence at the beginning—as something is setting out and taking shape— then even if the influence is small, it can go a very long way. The lessons we learn and examples that are internalized early on can affect us quite deeply.

Similarly, this works with how we apply the teachings. In particular, when we reflect on the cycle or chain of dependent origination—the laws of causality that govern our experience and the arising and ceasing of *dukkha*—we can see that the earlier in the chain that we catch this process of causality, the less work we have to do to uproot suffering. When we look at the way we handle the worldly winds—happiness and un- happiness, praise and criticism, success and failure, gain and loss—the mind can be observed reacting to and chasing after gain, running away from loss, identifying with, seizing hold of, and cherishing praise, rejecting criticism, and so forth. The sooner these reactive habits are seen and known, the less sor- row, lamentation, pain, grief, and despair we experience.

We live very much in our everyday world of perception and feeling. We see sights and hear sounds, touch objects, make decisions, engage with our bodies in the material world and with the 10,000 thoughts, moods, and ideas that arise from those various forms of sense contact. The more we internalize and make use of the teachings on dependent origination, the more we are aware that this is merely sense contact—*phassa*. Sense contact gives rise to pleasant, unpleasant, and neutral feelings—this is beautiful, this is ugly, this is ordinary. From that launchpad of feeling, in the ordinary flow of our experience, what arises is *taṇhā*, craving. *Vedanā paccaya taṇhā*—feeling conditions craving, which then leads to sorrow, lamentation, pain, grief, and despair. When we know this chain of causation, we are able to see that a feeling can easily turn into thoughts of *I can't stand this. This is wrong. This is bad. I don't like this. I have to get rid of it.* Or the opposite, *I want it. This is good. This is mine. I have to keep it, hold onto it, or own it.* When this cycle begins with possessiveness, we can see how that sense of ownership causes a feeling of loss, and then dukkha ensues.

Again, if we influence a three-year-old in a wholesome manner, those influences can have an effect for a lifetime. Similarly, if we mindfully catch the process right at the point where vedanā is conditioning taṇhā—feeling conditioning craving—the cycle can be broken right there. We can live with a heart completely at peace in the realm of feeling, and reflect, *This vedanā is present. I don't have to own it. Praise is sweet, criticism is bitter. Gain is sweet, loss is bitter. This is how it is. I don't need to make anything more of it than just that. This is the mind that likes sweetness, this is the mind that dislikes bitterness. That's all. It's empty. There's nothing there. It doesn't belong to me or anyone* else. *It's merely one of the attributes of nature coming into being, taking shape, and dissolving. That's all it is.* So the heart remains at peace, even though there's full engagement in the world of seeing, hearing, smelling, tasting, and feeling, as well as perceiving, doing, and acting. There's full engagement, but it is free of confusion and there is no identification with it.

If we catch the process even earlier, way down at the deep-tissue level, and mindfulness is sustained acutely, then ignorance—the whole duality of me as a person experiencing the world out there, of me here going somewhere else, the subject being the knower of the object—is not given any strength or substance. If we don't catch it, however, that is when *avijjā paccaya saṅkhāra*—ignorance conditions mental formations. When there is ignorance, then that duality of saṅkhāra or compoundedness arises. But if there is full awareness, full knowing, full mindfulness, then even that subtle degree of ignorance or delusion does not arise and is not given credence.

Discourses on dependent origination often state, "With the cessation of ignorance, there is the cessation of mental formations, and with the cessation of mental formations, there is the cessation of consciousness," and so forth. Phra Payutto points out in his book *Dependent Origination* that cessation is not meant to be taken only in terms of something beginning and then ending. The Pāli word for cessation is *nirodha*, which also implies *non-arising*. When there's no ignorance, then mental formations do not arise, the mind does not create the world of "thingness" or "this-and-thatness." This is the realization of Dhamma. It is simply Dhamma. It is not fabricated. It is not divided. It is not created. It is not split into me being here and the world out there—a subject separated from an object. This is the peace and clarity of realizing the Dhamma here and now.

Loving-Kindness and
Living in Harmony

Luang Por Pasanno • May 2005

The Buddha taught the *Saranīya Dhammas*, which are the six principles of conciliation or harmonious living. The first three of these Dhammas are based on bodily, verbal, and mental acts of loving-kindness. By generating loving-kindness, we create a strong condition for the arising of wholesome kamma. When we establish harmony with others, we build on that foundation of loving-kindness. The fourth Dhamma, which encourages sharing or giving, also has its basis in loving-kindness. When one is living together in a community as we do, this quality of sharing is essential to creating a sense of mutual congeniality and care. The fifth principal is virtue, which establishes trust—and thereby harmony—among people living together. When we trust each other, we have a sense of mutual loving-kindness as well. The last Saranīya Dhamma regards holding a noble view of the potential for freedom, the ending of suffering. When we see that we and others can realize this Dhamma, and that our companions have the same view, it creates feelings of kinship and kindness based on this harmonious perspective.

How do we bring up loving-kindness? What do we do when we feel it's impossible? When it does arise, what makes us lose it? The Buddha taught that loving-kindness is appropriate in all situations, so it is helpful for us to reflect on these questions and try to answer them for ourselves. By investigating, we can learn to encourage and sustain loving-kindness, work with it, and challenge any aversion we may have to it. This doesn't mean we'll get it right all the time, but we should reflect on how to bring about loving-kindness in our thoughts, actions, and speech, because it's through loving-kindness that we live in a harmonious way.

Perceiving the Unbeautiful

Ajahn Yatiko • July 2012

Yesterday Luang Por Pasanno spoke on the theme of *asubha kammaṭṭhāna*—contemplating the unbeautiful. This topic can be embarrassing for Westerners to talk about because it seems like such a foreign and strange concept, deeply personal and almost taboo. Why do we contemplate the unbeautiful? The answer isn't immediately obvious, but if we look at this question in terms of our own experience, we begin to see its benefit in our practice.

There is a strong tendency to judge and slap a perception on everything we experience, and it could be said that whatever we experience is filtered through these perceptions. In particular, we habitually distinguish objects as either beautiful or unbeautiful. There is something within us that creates this perception. But in fact, it's merely a perception, not the ultimate truth of things. We can perceive anything in the world as being beautiful or unbeautiful depending on the way we've been conditioned to look at it, but when we look at the body, we almost always see it as beautiful and ignore its unbeautiful features. That's our default bias. There is a deeply ingrained tendency toward creating and perceiving the beautiful in the body. We become attached to the beautiful, worry and fight about it, and become distressed when we lose it.

We all have *rāga-taṇhā*, sensual desire, as part of our being. If our parents didn't have rāga-taṇhā, we wouldn't be here.

When sensual desire is present, we want to perceive the beautiful in the body. When it's not present, the body doesn't seem so beautiful anymore—it doesn't appeal to us in the same way. We're no longer in the grip of a desire that can lead to painful mind states and regrettable behavior. This is where asubha practice comes in. When we start thinking about what comprises the human body—bones, sinews, blood, intestines, undigested food, the heart, the whole lot of it—we may come to realize that these objects have an unattractive quality to them.

When left to our own devices, we tend to only focus on the thin layer of skin that wraps around these unattractive objects, ignoring everything else. Or we convince ourselves that the skin is of a different nature than the rest of our body—but how could that be so? How could the skin be of a different nature? The unbeautiful quality of skin and of what it contains are exactly the same, but because we've created a fixed perception that the skin is beautiful, we see it in that way.

The fact is, nothing in the world is inherently beautiful or ugly. These are merely qualities we create and project onto the world. We can create an entire universe of perceptions around the beautiful and the ugly, which then dictate to us what we want or don't want. It becomes a heavy experience, a heavy reality, which is completely unnecessary. Asubha practice can help liberate us from this tyranny of entrenched perceptions.

Initially, there can be a strong resistance to asubha kammaṭṭhāna. This resistance is rāga itself—the desire that does not want to give up the perception of beauty. Recognizing and investigating this resistance can be very interesting and a profound experience in its own right as well as a direct way of working with fear. Even so, we might say to ourselves, *I didn't take up the Buddha's teachings to focus on the unbeautiful!* But actually, this is a significant part of the Buddha's teachings, and it doesn't in any way overshadow the beauty of those teachings. In fact, the feelings that arise from asubha practice are themselves quite beautiful—feelings of letting go, release, and freedom. It also helps in overcoming our resistance to recall that asubha practice is to be done within the supporting framework of loving-kindness toward ourselves and others.

However, we *do* need to apply this practice with discernment, to watch out for any difficulties that arise. If we find ourselves getting negative results from the practice, it's perfectly fine to put it aside for weeks, months, or even years if necessary. However, it's worth working with the difficulties, because asubha kammaṭṭhāna is such a potentially rewarding practice. Eventually, if we use this practice repeatedly, we will likely discover that it's an extremely useful tool for the realization of Dhamma.

What Do We Take With Us?

Ajahn Karuṇadhammo • August 2013

We can take this moment to let the momentum of planning for the morning settle before launching into the day. Watch the mind that's leaping forward to go and accomplish the tasks, to start the workday, to do what needs to be done. Watch the momentum of becoming—identifying with the various activities we're about to perform and the roles that we have— the ideas, thoughts, views, opinions, perceptions, conceptions. Watch how we identify with the activities and emotions of the mind.

A couple of days ago I went to visit a woman who was in the process of dying. She probably doesn't have too much longer to go now. She's someone who has always wanted to live life fully, being involved and engaged with many different good things. Like most of us, she's strongly identified with that and does not want to look closely at the dying process or what death means for her. When I saw her, she was at a point where her body was not responding to her wishes to keep it going. She wanted to continue living fully engaged and was trying to find gratification by doing all of the wholesome things she used to do, but her body was going counter to that. It was saying to her, "I'm packing it in" and it was no longer going to be a viable vehicle for living life fully. She is realizing all of this now.

When we have such a strong impulse toward becoming, identifying closely with the body, and then all of a sudden we're faced with the dying process—the body going in the ppo-site direction, the direction of non-becoming—then we can experience a very sudden wake-up call. The momentum of the mind toward using the body as a vehicle for identification, for becoming, for gratification is ripped out from underneath us when the dying process begins. What a lesson this can be for all of us.

This is why the Buddha suggested the contemplation of death as a necessary reflection for us. It helps us to uproot that sense of identification and the impulse we have toward becoming what or who we think we are, or what we identify with—our bodies, our activities, or our roles in the monastery. In the ordination process here, when we're long-term lay residents in the monastery, we look forward to becoming anagārikas. When we're anagārikas, we look forward to becoming sāmaṇeras. When we're sāmaṇeras we look forward to becoming bhikkhus. Then, when we're bhikkhus, we look forward to becoming ajahns. And then ... we're almost dead.

What is it that we can take with us? We can't take any of those identities or roles. We can't take any of the accomplishments with us nor can we take our failures. We can't take any of the praise we've received for things we've done well or the blame we've received for things we haven't done well. Whatever we have gained or lost doesn't go with us when we die. All of the status we've accumulated, all of our particular views about the way things should be run, all of the times we were able to be alone, wanting to escape from being around others, or all of the times we sought the company of others, being surrounded by family and friends—we don't take any of those with us. They all disappear when we die. All we take with us are the impulses and the tendencies we have toward either skillful states of mind like generosity, morality, and patience or the more unskillful impulses of greed, hatred, and delusion. These tendencies, in as much as we develop them, are taken with us, but we don't take any of the other things that we generally hold to as so important or permanent.

So throughout the day, what is it that we want to develop? If we're going to die tonight, what qualities do we want to take with us? Do we want to take the becoming tendencies, the activities, the momentum of tasks, identities and roles, how we think we are, how we want to be seen by other people, or how we present ourselves to the world? Do we want to work on those? Or do we want to work on developing the essential aspects of our practice: service, kindness, skillfulness, wisdom, discernment, patience, or energy? Those are the qualities, the tendencies we can take with us. The choice is up to us. We can choose the skillful tendencies leading us toward seeing this process of becoming, this process of how we identify with the body. And then we can learn how to let it all go. Or we can go in the opposite direction. It all depends on where we focus our attention as we move throughout the day.

Carrying It Around

Luang Por Pasanno • July 2012

We've had visitors from Thailand in the past four weeks, and I think it's important to have this kind of contact and connection with elder monks in our tradition. During this time, there's been a fair amount of coming and going, which has been conducive to a lot of busyness. Now we can allow the monastery to settle into a bit more simplicity—the simple rhythm of our daily duties, chores, and practices. We'll take the next bit of time to practice on our own in the evenings, giving each other the opportunity for a bit more space and solitude.

Sometimes we have space, but we just fill it up, distracting ourselves with socializing and chatting. This is a good time to get back to our *kuṭis* and keep that theme of simplicity going. We can sit in our kuṭis by ourselves, proliferating about all sorts of things, and miss that opportunity for inner simplicity. Alternatively, we can attend to the simplicity of watching the breath or doing walking meditation at our kuṭis and learn how to delight in that.

When the Buddha taught his aunt, Mahāpajāpatī about the Dhamma in brief, he emphasized non-proliferation or non-complexity as a characteristic that aligns itself with *Dhamma-Vinaya*, the teachings and the discipline. We can add our complications and complexities to everything around us. But if we remember to attend to the practice and maintain our focus, the practice will naturaly shed the complication and complexity.

We have a habit of carrying around all sorts of proliferations and complications. Because we believe in them, we invest in them. Just think of all that complexity—the planning of our lives, the worrying about an external event that may or may not happen, the carrying around in our minds of all the people in our social environment: *This person said that and that person said this,* and on and on it goes—it's endless. When we're caught up in those sorts of things, it's time to ask ourselves, *Is this really necessary? What's the point? If the Dhamma-Vinaya of the Buddha is for non-proliferation and non-complication, then why do I insist on carrying all that around? How do I put it down? How do I return to the principles of Dhamma-Vinaya and continue with the training?* A part of the answer is to give ourselves the time and space to practice at our dwelling places in the forest. Obviously, we still need to exercise skill when coming into contact with other people, but physical solitude is what helps develop the heart and mind. That's what we're here for, so let's focus on that.

Putting Aside What I Want to Do

Ajahn Yatiko • December 2012

In last night's Dhamma talk, Ajahn Karuṇadhammo said that one of the most valuable things we can do as residents of the monastery is develop generosity of heart by helping to create harmony in our community. Instead of looking at things solely from the perspective of what we like and what we want, we also consider the wants and needs of the group and what is best for everyone in the community. It is good to think of the Saṅgha as an organism of which we are a part.

There is a lovely passage that is often quoted from the suttas in which the Buddha is talking to a group of three monks living together, Venerables Anuruddha, Nandiya, and Kimbila (MN 31). When the Buddha asks how they cultivate harmony, Venerable Anuruddha says, "Well, Lord, I ask myself, *Why should I not put aside what I want to do and instead do what these venerable ones want to do?* Then I put aside what I want to do and do what they want to do."

It is true that while we are here we cultivate solitude. Solitude is an important part of our practice, but equally important is the need to ask ourselves, *What am I doing in solitude? Is it helping my practice or not? Am I cultivating wholesome, bright mind states in solitude, or might doing acts of service and helping the community be more beneficial for my mind?* We don't have to be out there all the time doing things, but whenever there is a possibility of helping the community or an individual, that is an excellent opportunity to say to ourselves, *Okay, here's my chance to do something, to break out of my mold of solitude and contribute to the life of the monastery.* For example, let's say I needed a volunteer to give me a hand with something outside of the work period this afternoon, and I asked, "Is anyone available for an hour?" In a situation like that, while we may have it in mind to get back to our cabin and do some sitting, have a rest, read some suttas or whatever, instead we could spontaneously drop that thought or desire and offer assistance. For this to be a special gift of generosity, it takes a willingness to be spontaneous—this is how it comes from the heart. To say to ourselves in the moment, *Sure, I'd be willing, I'll volunteer for that, I'd love to.* That's a beautiful way to create harmony and appreciation, and it's a fine example of the generosity that comes from the heart.

My intention is not to be one-sided. I'm not saying that solitude is not important and that as monastics and people living in the monastery, we don't have the duty to cultivate a love for solitude, but we should also remember that a love of generosity is an important part of the path.

I remember a time when a person who'd lived as a monk for ten or fifteen years was clearly going through difficult times and was suffering from serious mental problems. One of the senior Thai ajahns was talking about the reasons for this person's breakdown and said, "It's because he hasn't developed enough generosity in his practice." You could see that was true from this monk's behavior. He spent most of his time in solitude, but didn't do it in a skillful way. He tended to run off to be by himself at every opportunity. He rarely served or gave of himself. It is not as if other monks didn't want him in the monastery or didn't want to be around him. It was simply that they could not appreciate his presence, because he was never really there for anyone.

A community is like an organism that requires care, attention, and participation in order to function and remain beautiful, comfortable, pleasant, and healthy. As members of the community, each of us has to do our part in order to make that a reality, because it does not come about accidentally or on its own. In terms of cultivating the path, I think this is worthy of reflection for our daily practice.

Mindfulness Develops Right Speech

Ajahn Jotipālo • May 2013

Ajahn Dtoen came to visit us once, right after one of our winter retreats. During a question and answer period, I asked him if there were any exercises we could do to improve the wholesomeness of our speech or how to approach right speech as a practice. He saw right through me. He could see I was hoping there was some sort of technique I could apply before speaking that would solve all my problems around speech—a technique that would tell me when my speech was appropriate and timely. Ajahn Dtoen shook his head and said, "No, if you are looking for a method or a technique, it's too late. What you really need to be developing is all-around, all-encompassing mindfulness. For example, right now, where are your sandals? If you were mindful when you took them off you would know exactly where they are, what direction they are facing, and possibly whose sandals are next to yours."

After we've taken off our jackets or set our car keys down, if we don't know exactly where they are right now, we probably weren't mindful when we set them down. We can take that as a practice, a training. With everything we do we can try to make a mental note. That's one way to bring ourselves fully into the present moment. To do that we need to carefully slow down and be aware of the action we are doing. If we practice being aware of where we place our personal items, then as a benefit from that, we have trained ourselves to slow down and be aware of our mind states. When speech then comes into play, the mind can be more aware of what we are doing and we can start seeing what is appropriate or not appropriate—if this is the right time to speak or not. We may learn to question whether we need to say anything at all. By training in this way, the ability to discern and make judgments about speech can become much stronger because we have developed it with mindfulness.

How Do I Accord With Truth?

Luang Por Pasanno • May 2012

There's a tendency to look for some technique or method we can follow and perfect, whether it's for cultivating mindfulness, concentration, or whatever. This is helpful at times, but no matter what method or technique we're trying to develop, we always need to consider whether we're doing it within the framework of right view—whether we're doing it with a view that accords with Dhamma. If we're missing right view in the way we're applying and cultivating our practice, no matter what method or technique we use, we're going to complicate things and create difficulties for ourselves. So we need to keep turning attention inward and ask ourselves, *How do I accord with Dhamma? How do I accord with truth? How do I align myself with a view that's in accord with reality and in accord with the Buddha's perspective.*

Generally there are three ways we view experience: Being drawn toward the world, being drawn toward the sense of self, or viewing experience in accord with truth. Often we're entangled with, caught up in, or propping up the feeling of self or the views and opinions that arise from the sense of self. Or it's the pull toward the world, relying on the world as a source of gratification, energy, or interest. When we're aware of that happening, we can draw our attention back and ask ourselves, *How do I accord with Dhamma, with truth?* This is where that sense of right view is so important.

I remember a group of Buddhist teachers saying to Ajahn Chah, "We teach about right view. We've been studying about right view. But what the heck *is* right view, anyway?" Ajahn Chah smiled, held up the cup he was drinking from, and said, "right view is knowing that this is a broken cup. It's just that much." So we need to recognize the impermanence, uncertainty, and unsure nature of experience, rather than making assumptions about things from the bias of "my way" or from perceptions of the world as good or bad. We might think, *Everything is falling apart.* Or we might think, *Everything is great and I'm going to get what I want. The world is going to gratify me!* Well, not sure. We need to stop and reflect, *What is sure?* We may see that what *is* sure is what we can know at this present moment. What *is* sure is that we can make choices and try to guide ourselves in ways that are skillful.

When we make those choices, it is helpful to recollect that we are the owners of our actions, heirs to our actions, and that those actions have results. As soon as we formulate an idea, often something will come out of the mouth or we do something with the body. Those actions have consequences, good or bad. We need to take responsibility for that, recognizing the causal relationship between particular actions and their results. How do we attune ourselves to this cause-and-effect conditionality?

We can begin by asking ourselves, *What's going to lead to my well-being, happiness, and peace? How do I avoid this confusion, difficulty, and suffering?* And we can keep taking responsibility, reflecting over and over again, *I'm the owner of my actions, heir to my actions, born of my actions. Whatever actions I shall do, for good or for ill, of those I will be the heir.* But in order to take responsibility like this, we need to step back and clearly see that, *It's not sure. I don't have to believe my moods. I don't have to believe the world around me. I don't have to get caught in conditions. None of it is sure.* Once this sinks in, we can allow right view and the Dhamma to guide us, rather than allowing ourselves to be pulled by the conditions of the world or the conditions of identity and self view.

Self-Effacement

Ajahn Karuṇadhammo • December 2012

Developing insight around the aspect of *anattā*, not-self, is often understood to arise from a sudden insight, awakening, or penetration that results from the culmination of earnestly practicing *samatha* and *vipassanā*, concentration and insight. In a sense there's a truth to that. A deep and penetrating insight does come through investigation. But there's a slow, gradual process that can also lead to this insight of not-self. The word that describes this slower process best is *self-effacement*—a gradual thinning or wearing away of the self-making process, this sense of me and mine, and the ownership and identity around all the things we usually identity with. The process of self-effacement is a progressive and steady process, a whittling away over time through various practices, not only with the practice of meditation and development of insight around the three characteristics—suffering, impermanence, and not-self—but also with everything we do as part of community training. Many of the things that we incorporate into our daily lives and daily practices are ways of increasing this kind of self-effacement, this gradual diminishing of our sense of identity. It's a process that can take many, many years.

Dhamma practice and training, particularly in the monastic form, is a long-term endeavor. There are many ways that our structures and community life help support self-effacement. For example, the practice of generosity is an external way of reducing the sense of self-importance. We give of ourselves by offering our time and support to each other and by making an effort in how we communicate with one another. We are also generous with the work duties we take on and how we contribute around the monastery. Little by little, if done sincerely, it's all a part of the self-effacing process.

The hierarchy is another way that we can encourage this process. As much as we try to establish an environment where people feel comfortable to express themselves about the way things should happen, there's also the sense of hierarchy that we give ourselves to. We have business meetings and regular circle meetings where people contribute in a free way. When decisions need to be made, we utilize this hierarchy based on seniority. Basically, it's boiled down to one very simple aspect of who's been around the longest in robes. Hopefully, there's also a bit of experience and maturity that comes along with years in the robes, so it's not completely an arbitrary structure. Most importantly, it's also a way of learning to let go of self views, self opinions, or the thought, *My way is the right way.* If there's some sort of disagreement or something that needs to be worked out or decided on with different views and opinions, then seniority plays a part in that. We turn over a bit of selfishness to the monastery hierarchy. As Ajahn Yatiko was saying, if somebody misses a morning meeting, an evening meeting, work, or whatever other communal activity we have, then the proper protocol is to mention one's absence to the senior monk as a way of being open and honest. This is not encouraged as a punitive guilt trip, but as a way of acknowledging our mistakes. All of these actions add up little by little—working together, bumping up against each other, accommodating each other, giving up our own views and opinions—all of these are subtle ways of working toward self-effacement.

A number of us came to the monastery with a sense of wanting to become something or somebody. It's sometimes nice to develop a set of skills or a particular training that we can call our own, as a way of feeling like we can contribute something unique. That's not a bad intention, but it can sometimes be held to as an identity. For example, we might want to become the best work monk, the best guest monk, the best attendant, the best meditator, the best teacher, the most knowledgeable in suttas, or whatever it is that we want to identify with. All of these skills can be useful tools for community life, but we can also develop a sense of identity around them—becoming this or becoming that—and doing what we might be doing if we were engaged in worldly careers. The idea is to pick up all of these things, use them, develop skills around them, but do this for the purpose of maintaining community life and offering service, as well as for the purpose of learning how to give up self identity and a sense of self-importance within this same process. Little by little, bit by bit, with this process we're realizing that there really isn't any "me" here who's doing all of this. We are using skills to develop the Eightfold Path, to encourage each other, and to contribute to Saṅgha harmony. Gradually this process supports us in developing the insight into who we are not.

Remembering to Loosen Up

Ajahn Amaro • September 2008

By reflecting on the theme of kindness and establishing the quality of *mettā*, we gain insight into how mettā is developed. One of the not-so-obvious ways we create qualities of unkindness is by relating to our own attitudes, opinions, and pet projects through self-identification: *My responsibility, my job, my role.* Many of these aspects of our lives slip into existence and claim a substantial reality without our noticing. *Of course this is what I am. This is my job. I'm the water monk. I'm the co-abbot. I'm the head cook. I'm the driver. This is what I am.* The mind takes hold of these particular attitudes and creates a false substantiality around them. The more solid they become, the more we create the causes of friction.

If we want to sharpen a blade, we don't get a soft grindstone made of gelatin. We get a good, hard grindstone for the blade to rub against, something that's solid, unyielding, and abrasive. The more the mind hardens around opinions, the more we buy into them, creating false solidities and divisions between the apparent me and the apparent world. The more solid and unyielding these attitudes and opinions become, just like an abrasive grindstone, the more friction there is and the more sparks that fly.

Developing the quality of mettā, in terms of non-contention in the way that we behave and relate to others, is an important dimension to notice. We don't often think of this in terms of mettā practice, but it's helpful to bring a genuine attentiveness to the kind of fixedness, the sense of territoriality that the mind can have, or the fixedness of views that identifies with a particular role, position, or responsibility. *This is my position. This is my job. You do your thing and I'll do mine.*

I remember one of the nuns from Chithurst Monastery talking about her pre-nun life in the kitchen at Amaravati. She said, "It's quite incredible—the opinions about the ways to cut a carrot." She spent three years as an *anagārikā* at Amaravati, which has a kitchen about three or four times the size of the kitchen here at Abhayagiri, and at least ten times the number of opinions. People were almost coming to blows on occasions and stomping out of the house. "Those carrots have been cut wrong—it's completely out of order, inappropriate, and contrary to the Dhamma to cut carrots like that!"

We might not notice in the course of a day the 10,000 ways the mind creates a sense of territory, priority, or position, and seeks ways to establish them. We can be very polite, keep the precepts, and do things in the appropriate way, but at the same time send out signals that are based on identifying with a particular position. *I'm right. This is my job. You don't matter. What I'm doing is important. My views are correct. What you do is totally insignificant.* It's all the habits of self creating the *I* and *my*. We can take the ordinary, utterly innocent activities of our monastic lives—helping out with the work tasks, washing the dishes, putting things away in our cupboards, or whatever it might be—and use them to feed those I-creating, my-creating habits. It's useful to bring attention to that, to see where we create a fixedness of views and a false solidity. Then we can challenge our own opinions, habits, and preferences by training the heart into not buying into them, not going along with that kind of subtle grasping. And remember to loosen up! This is a genuine act of kindness. It's a kindness to ourselves not to create that sort of stress and fearfulness within our own hearts. It's also a great kindness to the people around us. They are much more able to harmonize with us when we're able to harmonize with them. There's less of the alienation that comes from clinging to self view and self-creating habits. We are no longer like a hard unyielding grindstone.

There are many different dimensions to developing mettā. We can see how much of a difference it makes when we notice within ourselves a hardening of the heart or a clinging to an opinion, belief, or preference, and then we change direction by relaxing around our views and loosening up our identification with those opinions and preferences. We experience for ourselves the blessings that come from the more easeful and pleasant world we live in because we're not vying for positions, judging each other, fearing being judged, or positioning ourselves against this or that person. Notice how delightful and wonderful it is to have none of that being created. We realize, *Oh look at that. If I don't create it, then it's not there. What an amazing surprise!* So much of the stress and difficulty of our personal worlds is generated from our own *cittas*, our own minds and hearts. If we ourselves stop creating that division and stress—that friction and heat from the grindstone—then we find the citta becomes cool because the division and tension simply aren't there.

One Who Sees the Danger in Saṃsāra

Luang Por Pasanno • May 2013

Contemplations and reflections on death and dying are a means of focusing attention, and prioritizing where we choose to put our attention. We can ask ourselves, *What is it we are becoming absorbed in? What are we letting the mind run away with?* These are essential contemplations because they help us make the practice—including relinquishment and generosity—our first priority.

The literal translation of the word *bhikkhu* is one who subsists on alms. But in keeping with the commentaries, Ajahn Chah used to emphasize that the meaning of *bhikkhu* is one who sees the danger in *saṃsāra*, the danger in the endless round of birth and death, the endless wandering. That's a useful image for the unfocused, inattentive mind—the mind that does not prioritize, that drifts aimlessly about. It wanders to moods of like and dislike, moods of resentment and attachment, and continues to wander on. This reflection on one who sees the danger in saṃsāra applies to everybody, not only monks. It can encourage us all to make good use of our faculties, to take the opportunities afforded to us through our bodies and our minds.

So we recollect and reflect on our impending death and the endless cycle of saṃsāra, in order to sustain our attention and to keep the practice as our first priority.

Happy to Stay at Home

Ajahn Yatiko • June 2013

One of the most important things for us to be doing here—as either monastics or as visiting laypeople living like monastics—is to develop our formal meditation practice. A key to this is learning how to delight in meditation—the freedom that comes from simply sitting, not becoming anything, resting in a state of mind that is able to put things down.

Yesterday I was reflecting on the word *concentration*, which is the most common translation for *samādhi*. I think that's a poor translation because concentration has a strong sense of coercing the mind, forcing it to be a certain way. My understanding of samādhi is that it is a freeing experience, rather than one which squeezes the mind into a frozen or held state of being. It is much more an experience that allows us to let go of unwholesome states of mind, especially those we are obsessed with or attached to. What remains is a mind that is relaxed, peaceful, and stable. It's not going out to search for happiness, because it is quite happy to stay where it is at home.

We often use the words *cultivating concentration*. which is an important expression, but it can be misleading. Quite simply, it means developing the ability to put things down. We can recognize that the things which we attach ourselves to are endless and that this attachment results in *bhavataṇhā*, a sense of becoming—the incessant inclination to exist, plan, create an identity, and attach to some idea of ourselves as some thing.

We're caught up in this becoming like an animal in a trap. Either we see that it's going to lead to suffering or we don't, but either way, if there's bhavataṇhā, suffering will be the result. One of the main tasks in our meditation practice is to learn how to put down this becoming. Once we do this, we will begin to experience a profound sense of freedom. As Sāriputta once commented to Ānanda, "Nibbāna is the cessation of becoming." We need to use our time here to not only develop service and generosity, which is so important to communal living and harmony, but also to pay attention to our formal meditation practice—sitting and walking—and developing the ability to put things down.

The Spider in Its Web

Luang Por Pasanno • October 2013

When the mind seeks objects for sense contact, it almost always finds the objects it seeks. When it seeks objects of stimulation, interest, gratification, aversion, or irritation, it can easily find them, because there's always something around to be excited or irritated about. That's why the quality of sense restraint is so important. We exercise this quality by paying close attention to the process of sense contact, and by learning to experience that contact—sights, sounds, smells, tastes, touch, and mental objects—without getting hooked into the desire and aversion, the liking and disliking that tends to happen when sense restraint is absent.

Ajahn Chah used the image of a spider sitting in the center of its web, alert and waiting. As soon as an insect touches the web, the spider goes out, grabs the insect, wraps it up, and brings it back to the web's center for eating. In a similar way, we have a web made from our senses and at its center is our heart and our ability to be aware. When this web is touched by some form of contact, we can draw that into the heart and—exercising sense restraint—we can reflect, investigate, and deal with that contact skillfully, according to Dhamma, without getting swept up in reaction and proliferation. When we take this quality of sense restraint as our center, we carry it into our daily lives of social interaction, duties and chores, and into formal meditation as well.

During the morning work period and at mealtime, we may let the mind get swept up into reactions and proliferations arising from social contact. Then, when we go back to our dwellings in the afternoon, the mind will be chewing on these same reactions and proliferations for perhaps hours, so that meditation becomes problematic. But if we are well established in sense restraint during such times of social contact, afterward the mind will be steady and stable—it will be in a state much more conducive to having a fruitful meditation. As we endeavor to establish continuity in our practice, we recognize sense restraint as a key aspect of that. Establishing a continuity of sense restraint ensures that the food in our web will be nourishing.

Unplugged Realities

Ajahn Karuṇadhammo • November 2013

I recently came back from a one-week visit to Tisarana Monastery in Ottawa, Canada to help them celebrate their kaṭhina ceremony. During this time I did a lot of traveling and spent some time in airports. While I was en route I noticed the alarming amount of people who were plugged into to one or another type of mobile device, either a smartphone, tablet, or laptop. It was interesting to observe them as each person seemed to be plugged into their own separate spheres or realities. They weren't interacting with others around them and seemed quite oblivious to what was happening in their surroundings.

One man I observed was conducting his business before boarding the plane. I watched him as he made several calls and did business over the phone. He would talk, conclude a conversation, and begin another one. It occurred to me how internally caught up he was in this reality of his, this sphere of a world he created. As the announcements for the plane departure began, it seemed that there was this subtle attention off in one corner of his mind and he was able to be in touch with the fact that he was about to board the plane. When it was his turn to board, he rose up but continued to speak on the phone, conducting business up until the very last point that he sat down on the plane and had to put his phone away.

I reflected upon this and thought about how, without cell phones or portable computers, we do much of the same thing here in the monastery. It is so easy to get caught up into our own realities and dwell in these separate spheres, absorbed in what we think is some permanent condition of the mind. We can get fixated upon some idea, mind state, or concern we have and not really see that it is a changing phenomena. It could be something like a health concern or some interaction we have with someone, and we believe this reality is all that exists for us. Our thoughts can revolve around this world to the degree that we are unable to see outside of this closed perspective or view.

Then, without even noticing it, some action outside of us or something someone says, completely distracts us from this world we have become so absorbed in, and we are reborn into this new world without even remembering what we were so obsessed with just moments ago. This new reality becomes the focus of attention in a way that can prevent us from seeing this entire process. It's as if we are jumping from one world to the next with no fixed point of reference. We can be blown around by our feelings, thoughts, and preoccupations about these insubstantial experiences.

Even right now, as I end this talk, we are all going to get up, begin cleaning dishes, and prepare for the work period. This will be a completely different experience from what we are having right now. If we can be aware of this changing of worlds and not get so caught up with it, then we have the opportunity to see this blinding process and wake up to the understanding that there is something outside of our very fixed perspectives. We can learn to expand the view and have a spaciousness that can encompass our experiences from a much broader context. By doing this, we allow ourselves to see things quite differently, from a less absorbed and less self-focused point of view. When we expand the view like this, we have the opportunity to see how our minds are moving from one reality to the next, creating world after world. We can step back from that process and watch it from a centered but detached point of view. When this occurs, there is the possibility of stopping, ending this cycle of world hopping, and opening ourselves up to the reality of our present experiences.

Priming the Mind

Luang Por Pasanno • November 2012

As we get into the cool season, there are things around the monastery that need to be taken care of and chores that need to be finished before the winter retreat begins. It's a good time to be paying attention to all that, as well as trying to keep things fairly quiet.

Last week, during the Thanksgiving Retreat, I didn't really have a plan in mind for what I was going to teach. I ended up talking a lot about *anicca, dukkha,* and *anattā*—impermanence, unsatisfactoriness, and not-self—and how these three characteristics display themselves in our practice and how central they are. We constantly use reflections on the three characteristics when investigating our experience. This is not a contemplation we only do on retreat or during a time of formal meditation; it's an investigative perspective that we bring to all of our experience, both in formal practice, as well as in the day-to-day application of our mindfulness and contemplative living.

It is quite essential in the practice to bring that investigation into the mind, so that the mind is seeded or primed. Yesterday evening at teatime, we were talking about a video used to demonstrate a psychological phenomenon. It shows a circle of people passing two basketballs around. Some people in the group are wearing black and the others are wearing white. One ball is being passed between the players wearing black and the other ball is being passed between the players wearing white. The people viewing the video are told to keep track of the number of times the ball gets passed between the players wearing white. As a result, viewers focus on the players in white shirts and the ball to the exclusion of most everything else. So when somebody in the video dressed in a gorilla suit walks through the group of people throwing the basketballs, beats his chest, and walks off, most people don't even notice!

That's because the mind was primed to focus in a particular way—a way that produced an overall state of heedlessness. But if we prime the mind to view experience in terms of anicca, dukkha, and anattā, in terms of these universal characteristics, then we start to see those characteristics more consistently and clearly. However, we usually tend to overlook those fundamental truths of existence, thereby missing the big picture. We get caught up in our personal stories, worries, fears, likes, and dislikes. So we need to prime the mind for viewing our experience through the lens of Dhamma, because otherwise we overlook it. That's very much a part of our training in mindfulness, reflection, and investigation—keeping a particular agenda in mind.

Of course, the agenda here is to see how the Buddha's fundamental truths actually apply to our experience, how those truths affect us. The beneficial effects of seeing these truths are clarity, relinquishment, and loosening the grip of clinging and delusion. By priming the mind to see though the lens of Dhamma we are supporting wholesome inclinations toward spiritual truth and spiritual peace, rather than unwholesome inclinations that spur the mind into keeping us clouded in delusion.

The Reason We're Here

Ajahn Yatiko • December 2012

What is the whole point of our being here? Where do we expect the cessation of suffering to be? Is it some sort of project we're working on? Is that where the cessation of suffering is going to be found? When the fault-finding mind obsesses over other people's behavior, or when we find fault with ourselves, is that where suffering ceases? Take a look at where the mind goes and becomes contracted. Ask yourself, *Is this where the cessation of suffering is going to be found?* Because that's the reason we're here—to understand that. Be really clear and try to bring that to mind—I often remind myself of this. Whatever problem or issue it is that I'm obsessing over, I say to myself, *I didn't become a monk to solve a bunch of mundane, external problems.* What we need to focus on in our practice is much more important than that. When we reflect on the real reason we're here, the mind relaxes and steps back from the things it obsesses over. That's the state of letting go. We learn to apply it to all the different obsessions that come up in the mind, all the different activities and projects we focus on and become obsessed with.

Of course, projects do have to be done, and we do have to plan for things. But when we get caught up in all of it, that's what leads to suffering. We've lost our balance; we've temporarily lost contact with the whole purpose of our living here. At the same time, it isn't helpful to get down on ourselves for losing the plot—losing the plot happens to everyone. But in order to snap out of it, we need to be reminded of our purpose, which is to end suffering. We need to know that this is a possibility, and we have to bring our mindfulness to that issue so that we can loosen our grip around these different obsessions of the mind and stop wasting precious time. By doing this over and over again, we can learn to let go and realize that there's no reason to suffer.

Knowing Wholesome and Unwholesome States

Luang Por Pasanno • May 2012

The work period and the regular chores we have in the monastery are an extension of our practice. It's important to consciously bring that point to mind. Otherwise, it's easy to fall into the habit of being wrapped up in the excitement and enthusiasm we feel about the work project we are doing or being indifferent and waiting for the work period to be over. Whatever perceptions and attitudes we may have regarding the chore we're doing, it's essential to take that chore as an opportunity for establishing and sustaining our mindfulness. This is done with the help of *yoniso manasikāra*, skillful or wise attention.

As we were having tea, I spoke about the importance the Buddha placed on yoniso manasikāra. Its function is to direct attention in an alert and discerning way, no matter what we may be doing. Without yoniso manasikāra, we tend to get caught up in proliferation, in a mood, or in reactivity, because we haven't been attending closely to the situation.

The Buddha often described wise attention as knowing when there are wholesome states present in the mind, and knowing when there are unwholesome states present. It's also a quality that supports right effort—generating the wholesome and discouraging the unwholesome. To help with that, wise attention serves as an anchor for our mindfulness. I tend to encourage mindfulness of the body—using the body as a foundation for mindfulness and awareness, and for directing attention skillfully.

As we go through the work period and throughout the day, we can try to carry our attention in a clear and discerning way. Once we develop a continuity of wise attention, it will become a firm foundation for all of our growth in the practice.

Uncertainty:
The Spillway for the Mind

Ajahn Amaro • November 2008

With our friend Jay's health in such a precarious condition, this is a good time to reflect on uncertainty. Ajahn Karuṇadhammo was saying, "The doctors and nurses keep telling me that Jay can't last much longer. But I've seen so many times when, against all reason and medical possibilities, people continue to survive for a long time." This simple recollection can be helpful. We don't know how much longer Jay will be with us. Similarly, with the work scene, we don't know where the water tank leak is or even if there is a leak. We don't know if all the different work crews will get where they're supposed to this morning. We don't know if Jim will be attacked by fronds of poison oak. *We don't know.*

Throughout the course of any day, there are thousands of different situations either on the grand scale, like someone's life ending, or on the minuscule level—*Where have I left that hammer? What am I going to make to go with the broccoli? Who is driving the truck up the mountain?* We don't know. Instead of feeling frustrated because we're anxious and without a plan, we simply can recognize, *I don't know where that tool is, what to make with the broccoli, or who is driving. I don't know what's going to happen next or if this is going to work. I don't know.* We are bringing that quality of not knowing into our attention, rather than trying to get some information so we *can* know, or feeling frustrated or anxious because we don't have a plan or haven't figured out a particular problem. When we reflect on not knowing, we are letting go of our incessant need to ameliorate uncertainty—that refuge we usually take in making sure that everything has a plan, an answer, or some worldly solution.

Ajahn Chah would often say that this reflection on uncertainty is the flag or emblem of the Noble Ones. He would also say it's like a spillway for a dam. When we build a dam, we need to have a spillway to relieve the pressure and divert the excess water. Ajahn Chah would say, "Uncertainty is the spillway for the mind." That's what relieves the pressure in our lives and in our experience of the world.

So remember: It's uncertain, we don't know. When the mind makes a judgment, calling this good or bad, right or wrong, we can reflect, *Is it really a good thing? Don't know. Is it a bad thing? Don't know.* When we cultivate that reflection on uncertainty from a place of wisdom rather than from a place of self view and anxiety, it can serve as a spillway that relieves the pressure. Right there we can feel the relief in the heart. Often we think, *Oh, this is going to be great, now I'll be happy, everything is going to work out.* When thoughts like that arise, we need to follow them up with wisdom, *How presumptuous to believe I could know that. Of course, I don't know.* By frequently reflecting in this way, we can learn to stop looking for certainty in that which is intrinsically uncertain. What a relief.

As the day proceeds and we go about our work tasks, bear in mind that *we don't know.* Has Jay passed away? Is he still alive? Is he still breathing? *Don't know.* Whether it's concerning Jay or concerning the tasks at hand, notice how the quality of the mind depends on whether or not we're seeing uncertainty in relation to whatever judgment or activity is taking place. When we see uncertainty clearly—the uncertain nature of our lives—we directly experience the qualities of relief and ease.

Glossary

ajahn (Thai): Literally, "teacher." From the Pāli word ācariya; often used in monasteries as a title for senior monks or nuns who have been ordained for ten years or more.

anagārika: Literally, "homeless one." An eight-precept male postulant who often lives with bhikkhus and, in addition to his own meditation practice, also helps with certain services that are forbidden for bhikkhus to do, such as, using money, cutting plants, or cooking food.

anattā: Not-self, ownerless, impersonal.

anicca: Impermanent, inconstant, unsteady. Ajahn Chah often translated it as "not sure."

asubha: Unattractive, not-beautiful. The Buddha recommended contemplation of this aspect of the body as an antidote to desire, lust, and complacency.

bhikkhu: A Buddhist monk; a man who has given up the householder's life to join the monastic Saṅgha. He follows the Dhamma-Vinaya (the doctrine and discipline), the teachings of the Buddha as well as the Buddha's established code of conduct.

brahmavihāra: The four sublime or divine abodes that are attained through the development of mettā, karuṇā, muditā, and upekkhā (boundless loving-kindness, compassion, sympathetic joy, and equanimity).

Buddha: The historical religious leader and teacher who lived around 2500 BCE in the Ganges Valley of India. After his enlightenment, he established a monks', nuns', and lay community under the instruction of what he called the Dhamma-Vinaya—the doctrine and discipline. The word Buddha literally means "awakened one" or "enlightened one."

defilements: Impurities, vices. Unwholesome mental tendencies or inclinations that cloud the mind. In their most basic forms they are greed, hatred, and delusion.

Dhamma (Sanskrit: Dharma): In general, a spiritual or philosophical teaching describing the natural state of reality. When used in this book, Dhamma specifically refers to the teachings of the Buddha: a systematic understanding of suffering, its cause, and how one applies oneself to eliminate this suffering, thus ending the cycle of rebirth.

dhamma: Used as a term to define natural phenomena of the world, including phenomena of the mind.

Dhamma-Vinaya: The Doctrine and Discipline. The name the Buddha gave to the religion he founded. The conjunction of the Dhamma with the Vinaya forms the core of the Buddhist religion.

dukkha: "Hard to bear," unsatisfactoriness, suffering, stress.

Eightfold Path: See Noble Eightfold Path.

Forest Tradition: The tradition of Buddhist monks and nuns who have primarily dwelled in forests emphasizing formal meditation practice and following the Buddha's monastic code of conduct (Vinaya).

Four Noble Truths: The first and central teaching of the Buddha about dukkha, its origin, cessation, and the path leading toward its cessation. Complete understanding of the Four Noble Truths is equivalent to the realization of Nibbāna.

kamma (Sanskrit karma): Volitional action by means of body, speech, or mind. Kamma always leads to an effect (kamma-vipāka).

Kaṭhina: A traditional cloth offering ceremony held at the end of the annual Rains Retreat celebrating community harmony.

khandhas (Sanskrit skandha): Heap, group, aggregate. Physical and mental components of the personality and of sensory experience in general. The five bases of clinging: form, feeling, perception, mental formations, and consciousness.

kuṭi: A small dwelling place for a Buddhist monastic; a hut.

Luang Por (Thai): Venerable Father, Respected Father; a friendly and reverential term of address used for elderly monks.

Māra: Evil, craving, and death personified as a deity, but also used as a representation of these elements within the mind.

mettā: Loving-kindness, goodwill, friendliness. One of the four brahmavihāras or sublime abodes.

Middle Way: The path the Buddha taught between the extremes of asceticism and sensual pleasure.

mindfulness: See sati.

Nibbāna (Sanskrit Nirvāṇa): Final liberation from all suffering, the goal of Buddhist practice. The liberation of the mind from the mental effluents, defilements, the round of rebirth, and from all that can be described or defined. As this term also denotes the extinguishing of a fire, it carries the connotations of stilling, cooling, and peace.

Noble Eightfold Path: Eight factors of spiritual practice leading to the cessation of suffering: right view, right intention, right speech, right action, right livelihood, right effort, right mindfulness, and right concentration.

Observance Day (Thai: Wan Phra): Once a week in Thai monasteries, monks and lay people set aside work duties and devote their time for a day (and sometimes all night) to formal practice. If the practice is continued until dawn the next day, the monks and laity will often refrain from lying down until dawn.

Pāli: An ancient Indian language related to Sanskrit. The teachings of the Theravada school of Buddhism were transmitted orally in Pāli for hundreds of years before being written down at the beginning of the Common Era in Sri Lanka.

Pāli Canon: The standardized collection of Theravada Buddhist suttas written in the Pāli language.

paññā: Wisdom, discernment, insight, intelligence, common sense, ingenuity. One of the ten perfections.

pāramī (Sanskrit: pāramitā): Perfection of the character. A group of ten qualities developed over many lifetimes: generosity, virtue, renunciation, discernment, energy/persistence, patience or forbearance, truthfulness, determination, goodwill, and equanimity.

paritta: Literally, "protection." Auspicious blessing and protective chants typically recited by monastics and sometimes lay followers as well.

pūjā: Literally, "offering." Chanting in various languages typically recited in the morning and evening by monastic and lay followers of a particular teacher, in this case the Buddha. Typically these recitations pay homage to the Buddha, Dhamma, and Saṅgha.

Rains Retreat (Vassa): The traditional time of year that monks and nuns determine to stay in one location for three months. Some monastics will take this time to intensify their formal or allowable ascetic practices. Monks and nuns will refer to themselves as having a certain number of Rains Retreats which signifies how many years they have been in robes.

right effort: One factor of the Eightfold Path which describes how a practitioner endeavors to prevent or abandon unwholesome qualities as well as maintain and develop wholesome qualities within the mind.

right speech: One factor of the Eightfold Path describing the proper use of speech: refraining from lying, divisive speech, abusive speech, and idle chatter.

right view: The first factor of the Eightfold Path. Right view is seeing experience in terms of Dhamma. This requires an understanding of kamma—that there are wholesome actions, unwholesome actions, and results of those actions. In the highest or noble sense, to have right view means to completely understand the Four Noble Truths.

samādhi: Concentration, one-pointedness of mind, mental stability. A state of concentrated calm resulting from meditation practice.

sampajañña: Clear comprehension, self-awareness, self-recollection, alertness.

saṃsāra: Literally, "perpetual wandering." The cyclical wheel of existence. The continuous process of being born, growing old, suffering and dying again and again, the world of all conditioned phenomena, mental and material.

Saṅgha: This term is used to conventionally describe the community of ordained monks and nuns practicing the teachings of the Buddha. However, from a noble or ideal view, it specifically describes the followers of the Buddha, lay or ordained, who have realized one of the four levels of awakening: stream-entry, once-returning, non-returning, or Nibbāna.

saṅkhāra: Formation, compound, fabrication; the forces and factors that form things (physical or mental), the process of forming, and the formed things that result. Saṅkhāra can refer to anything formed by conditions, including thought-formations within the mind.

sati: Mindfulness, self-collectedness, recollection, bringing to mind. In some contexts, the word sati when used alone refers to clear-comprehension (sampajañña) as well.

sīla: Virtue, morality. The quality of ethical and moral purity that prevents one from engaging in unskillful actions. Also, the training precepts that restrain one from performing unskillful actions.

five spiritual faculties (pañc'indriya): Faith, energy, mindfulness, concentration, and wisdom.

sutta (Sanskrit sūtra): Literally, "thread." A discourse or sermon by the Buddha or his contemporary disciples. After the

Buddha's death the suttas were passed down in the Pāli language according to a well established oral tradition and finally committed to written form in Sri Lanka just around the turn of the common era. The Pāli suttas are widely regarded as the earliest record of the Buddha's teachings.

taints (āsava): Mental effluents, fermentations, or outflows. Four qualities that taint the mind are sensuality, views, becoming, and ignorance.

Triple Gem: The Threefold Refuge: the Buddha, Dhamma, and Saṅgha.

tudong (Thai): The practice of wandering in the country and living on alms food.

Upāsikā Day: A day for Abhayagiri lay devotees to visit the monastery and partake in an afternoon teaching.

Vinaya: The Buddhist monastic discipline or code of conduct. The literal meaning of Vinaya is "leading out," because maintenance of these rules leads out of unskillful states of mind. The Vinaya rules and traditions define every aspect of the bhikkhus' and bhikkhunīs' way of life.

Visuddhimagga: A post-canonical collection compiled by the Bhikkhu Bhadantācariya Buddhaghosa in the fifth century. It is a treatise explaining in detail the path of purification.

wat (Thai): A monastery.